MW01118682

Joyful Passage

A Woman's Path to Retirement

Copyright 2021 by Joan B. Reid

For Mom

Acknowledgements

Thank you, Judy Casillo, for your friendship and professional editorial guidance. Both have been invaluable for this project.

Thank you, my daughter, Tina, for all your suggestions, encouragement, and patience.

Thank you to the women who shared their personal retirement stories: Barbara, Charlotte, Joy, and Sharon. Thank you for your love and friendship.

Thank you for advance praises:
Nancy Hartney, author of *If You Walk Long Enough.*
Reverend Ruth R. Wainwright, M.A, M.Div.
Joan Y. Edwards, M.A., B.S., author of
Flip Flap Floodle, and *Joan's Elder Guide.*

Introduction

Work-to-retirement is like parentheses bracketing a beginning and an ending.

Your path to retirement may or may not be linear. Just as experiences can be different one day to the next, so are daily retirement experiences. Just as our careers have been different from one another, so will be retirement.

Your work journey may have started as a supermarket cashier, a secretary, babysitter. You may have earned several college degrees and were gradually promoted to manager, executive, or director. Maybe you are a successful entrepreneur, a teacher, lawyer. Regardless, now several decades later you are at the threshold of an enormous change.

My journey went from fulltime work to semi-retirement to retirement. This has been an ongoing process which began in 2014. During the transitions, I reflected on the uplifting occurrences, illness and accidents, belly laughs, dull and painful days, faith, and enlightenment.

In its totality a: Joyful Passage.

Rebirth

All birth is unwilling. Pearl S. Buck

It happened unexpectedly. Time crept without fanfare but became evident when I reached the age of 60. That's when I began to contemplate if retirement could be in my future. I didn't feel old, yet the calendar didn't lie and neither did the mirror. Past being a woman of "certain age" I was now facing a new reality. I may have to leave the cubicle *womb*.

With enrollment numbers falling at the college and colleagues who were fired one after the other, I kept one foot in the work world while the other foot stretched across the widening fissure to retirement. It would take one misstep to fall into an emotional and financial abyss. *Better to make a conscious choice than to leave things to chance,* I reasoned.

It proved to be a difficult transition to even think about. I harbored the usual fears about retirement: lost identity, less money, no social connection, boredom, and mortality. Work it seemed had provided an illusion and a buffer that if I continued to work the status quo would remain and so would I.

The work ethic runs deep through my soul. I began working like many of us at the age of sixteen. After college I hop-scotched through several career paths including banking, education, public relations, publishing, and most recently I was a college financial aid counselor. God, I am employable! I have skills enough for several lifetimes. Alas, I have one life, and hopefully one retirement to enjoy. And so do you.

My fears of lost status and less revenue won out for another two years until I reached the early retirement age of 62. It was to be a gradual change that worked for me, a 3-day work week (27 hours) which delighted my employer to have an experienced financial aid counselor who would continue to the do the same job in less time, for less money, and no benefits.

Regardless, the two days off each week proved to be eye-opening, scary, funny, and beautiful. This little difference brought enormous gains and helped me further into my passage to retirement. The decrease in pay was also catalyst for me to begin collecting social security.

"What will you do on your days off?" One overly concerned twenty-something colleague inquired. *Oh dear*, I thought, *she feels sorry for me.* I surprised her and myself when I replied, "I'm going to live my life."

"Live your life?" Another young colleague repeated.

How will I be alive? As if not working is not living. I quickly rattled-off a laundry list of activities such as walking, ride my bicycle, create collages, play tennis, chat with friends, sleep-in, stay-up late, volunteer, garden, read, make love in the afternoon, try new recipes, spend a day in complete silence or prayer.

What are or will be the circumstances surrounding your retirement decision? The organization or company you're at may be downsizing, merging, your coworkers have left or retired, your workload is increasing, all your colleagues were born after 1980; you're tired of the routine, routine, routine. Everyone's situation is different but arrives to the same question: Is it time for me to retire? Why and how you make that decision is unique to you alone, just as your retirement years can be.

Forget the platitudes: "The golden years." "This is the first day of the rest of your life." Does anyone even say these anymore? I decided to rejoice being 62 because I had become more grounded, wiser, and a bit zanier. I was ready for anything novel, chaotic, exotic, playful, challenging, and serene. Little did I realize that I was about to encounter each of these. Take a deep breath and just place your toe into the retirement water. You will be scared and exhilarated just as I was. There is no glass ceiling in retirement. Give yourself a promotion—retire.

Truth: Before I took my first step, I decided to consult with a counselor.

Professional Input

Know Thyself.
Socrates

I have always trusted that someone else has a better answer than I. A person who is trained to counsel others, lends a sympathetic ear, weighs all the facts, and pulls out a solution from the proverbial magic hat. That is why I consulted a well-known social worker in my area, an older woman with counseling credentials, someone who would understand me.

I called her at a low valley in my day and probably sounded depressed, almost desperate. She returned the call within a few hours and we spoke briefly about what I needed to discuss. She told me to come see her the very next day. This *really* was serious, and I needed professional help.

The very next day I went to her home office at exactly 4 PM, we sat facing one another, smiled, did a little small talk, and eventually targeted my concerns. The counselor sat quietly, did not take any notes, but I could tell she was assessing my demeanor and what I said. I explained that I was considering semi-and/or-full retirement because the college's enrollment had dropped, and the salary loss could be recouped with freelance writing. But wasn't sure if I was ready for retirement psychologically speaking.

As soon as I sat back in my chair, she launched into a diatribe of what was the big deal, if you don't like your job, leave it, and start free-lancing. "That's what I do," she continued. "In order to get work as a part-time musician, I have to make cold calls, audition; people aren't just going to hand over assignments to you." *Ouch.*

Her lack of empathy and understanding left me thunderstruck. She didn't seem to grasp how I was in a crisis, at the threshold of a life-changing event. This wasn't about merely quitting a job and finding a new one. I wanted to stop working fulltime...forever. This was HUGE for me. Someone who had worked fulltime most of her adult life, knew little of self-employment, had always worked for large corporations and organizations. There were pieces of me scattered in Bergen County, New Jersey, and

Rockland County, New York. My personal history, friendships, new beginnings, and farewell parties all had left indelible imprints. This was my life, and I wasn't sure that I could walk away from a life that I knew which had brought structure as well as income.

I was quiet for the most part, some from shock at her tone and words, and partly because I wanted to leave her office as quickly as possible, never to return. My eyes welled, and I kept nodding in agreement with whatever she said. I still don't recall all that she communicated, and maybe that's a good thing.

"So," she began to summarize, "Joan, you really **don't** need counseling. You just need to make a decision." That cost me $100.

I shook her hand, rushed out the door to my car and raced away. But my takeaway was this: that only I could decide for myself when and how to retire. No one could make that decision for me. Of course, this is not exactly how things turned out. This was just the beginning of the journey to a joyful passage.

The Leap

...the other side of every fear is freedom
Marilyn Ferguson

My husband and I are not one of those couples with gorgeous gray hair, walking along the beach laughing. We don't have a vacation home or even a first home. We do have disposable time because there are fewer chores in a 1-bedroom apartment. I don't know about you, but I'm tired of reading the bazillion online articles that warn not to start taking social security too soon.

Too soon means when you're actually eligible to start at age 62. *Conventional wisdom* has repeatedly told all of us that we should keep working. That's right, continue to rise at 6 AM in the dark during the winter, face the commuter traffic, keep those long hours in front of the computer, answering emails, inputting data, spitting out reports, going to meetings. Or if your job is physical, keep lifting those loads, the heavy machinery, freezing outside, sweating inside, and standing on your feet. Not to start collecting social security when you're eligible is like telling someone not to open presents on their birthday.

Those darn retirement stats really bother me. *They* urge that you run an inventory of your assets before retirement. Crunch numbers, tally expenses, revenue flow, and consider the what ifs. Please raise your hand if you have saved a million dollars for your retirement. Just as I thought.

Well, I did do my homework. I went to the Social Security web site and applied online. Spoke to my husband and my employer. Listed on a folded piece of paper were bills on one side and revenue on the other. The surprising revelation was this could work. Retirement could really happen. Never once had I dreamed reaching an age where retirement was on the table.

The next warning on the "Do Not Retire Early List" is that you'll spend too much. Would that include my first semi-retirement day purchase of two juice glasses that were on sale at Pier One? The total transaction was $3.46. At 11 AM a friend and I met at Panera's to celebrate her birthday and my new season. We each spent under $6 and enjoyed two hours of conversation. I was exhausted and hadn't even been semi-retired for 24 hours.

Later, my husband brought home a bright magenta Gerbera Daisy in a clear bowl filled with water to create soothing natural beauty. We talked and he told me how happy he was that I had two free days during the week. My goodness the first day has flown and it isn't even over yet. I may go for a walk, start dinner, listen to music or nap. Maybe I'll do them all...or nothing. Yes, that is what I'll do.

Is Semi-Retired Really Retirement?

Be happy in work—this is a gift from God.
Ecclesiastes 5:19

Thank goodness I still have a job. Being semi-retired is tricky business. There are so many choices of activities when I'm home that sometimes I just do nothing. Today, I'm back at the job from 9 – 4:30. My colleagues ask me how my day-off went. *Day-off?* I purposely don't remind them of my semi-retirement status and that after today I'm already looking forward to a 3-day weekend. Life is good. I had an extremely satisfying and relaxing first day. Retirement feels like being let out of school for summer vacation. It is amazing freedom.

I downplayed it and simply went to my cubicle and clocked-in on the computer. When I'm on the clock I can be paid up to 15 minutes of personal time. Having always been salaried I wonder did I need to clock-out to go to the bathroom or make a cup of tea. No worries. I'm at the same job. I'll do what I always did—work non-stop and eat lunch "al-desko" as the younger generation has coined. Sound familiar?

For a while I am disoriented; semi-retirement is like leading a double life. I don't want to rile my colleagues by being too cheerful, is that why I am depressed today? I look at the clock. It is 9 o'clock and if I had been home I may take a walk, then a quick shower. Read the paper, check for the mail. Wait…is this why I have worked since I was 16?   I can hear one of my dearest friends saying, "It is what it is." So now I'm sad because not only am I here at the job for the next 8 hours, but I realize when I'm home the activities are mundane.

Surely it is too early in retirement for me to make an accurate judgment, which is to say the same for you. Hold-off on evaluating your retirement for a while. Try not to monitor it too closely. Just as you shouldn't keep checking whether a baking cake has risen, don't keep questioning whether you're having fun yet. If you're semi-retired be grateful for the work, and on the free days, savor them whatever the activities or lack thereof. Retirement has peaks and valleys, only more peaks.

What Will You Be When You Grow Up?

*It takes courage to grow up
and become who you really are.*
e.e.cummings

When I was a child I wanted to be a doctor. My mother said that I could be a nurse. In my teens, I volunteered as a "Candy Striper" once each week after school. I wore a pink and white striped uniform and delivered meals to patients. Later I wanted to be a writer. Mom asked, "Why a writer?"

I eventually majored in psychology at college and after graduation did nothing remotely related to psychology unless you count the customers I encountered at my first job as a bank teller. As years passed I wore the hats of wife, mother, teacher, assistant editor, public relations director, feature writer and financial aid counselor. I never became a doctor. I never stopped writing.

What am I? Who am I? That is exactly what life's journey has been, and we should treat retirement no differently. It's just more of the journey of self-discovery. Some of us still don't know what we want to be when we grow up. Do you?

While I'm working on that, please don't label me an active senior, or even a super-senior. Don't tell me I'm spry, look good for my age, or that I'm an inspiration. Nor am I cranky, pessimistic, a nosey neighbor, or a negative nay-sayer. There is a world of choices for other ways to live. We should not feel as if we have stopped growing just because we're not learning that new computer application, revised procedure, or policy at a paying job. Don't settle for labels that others have invented, create a unique identity for yourself, nurture the new you. Retirement is not an end. It is a beginning.

Memory

*Happiness is nothing more than
good health and a bad memory.*
Albert Schweitzer

One of the challenges you may find in retirement is keeping track of the days. When you look outside, it doesn't look like a specific day of the week. The sun has risen and the sun sets.

My husband said since I started semi-retirement he can't keep the days of the week straight. I simply told him that Tuesday is my new Monday as well as a virtual Friday before Wednesday is my next day off. Simple.

Days that meld into weeks then months and seasons are not limited only to retirement. Young workers with so much on their plate can lose track of days and time. You may recall how work weeks sprawled across the year with little distinction except for the golden weeks of freedom known as vacation. Remember, vacation where you checked your work email once, twice, sometimes three times each day? Or the week away with the family while you were conferenced-in at a meeting? Oh, that week, now you remember. Well forget that now.

Retirement days may or may not be memorable, but every day is yours. You oversee the activities and direction of your life. I do encourage you to keep track of the days so you can keep to your plans and goals. But not because on Friday the report is due and your boss wouldn't mind having it on Thursday; or

Monday morning is the weekly staff meeting, or Wednesday marks the middle of the work week.

You may want a wall calendar, or a desk calendar, or use the one on your phone to note appointments, lunch, and dinner dates, or simply jot down what you're going to do that day. I bet none of us, retired or not, could recall what we ate for dinner last Tuesday unless it was a special occasion.

Today is Saturday. I'm going to do something that I usually do on Saturday as if I only have a Saturday to do it: the laundry and food-shopping. Except this Saturday my daughter will visit when she seldom comes on a Saturday. Whereby her visit set in motion a series of days where I wasn't sure which day it was.

But I do remember preparing homemade vegetarian burgers, a basil salad and sweet potato.

The point is memory does fail me sometimes. The words don't flow as easily, the hearing is fading a bit, my waist is thicker, but I'm relatively healthy. Nothing is perfect and neither is memory. The over-arching sweeping memory you want to recall when you look back at retirement is, "It was a wonderful time in my life."

You May Retire Lakeside,
but Retirement is a Vast Ocean
J.B.Reid

Have you ever sat on the beach looking out to the horizon, wondering what is beyond your vision? The waves hypnotically lull you into a trance where your mind wanders in and out of rooms searching, for what? An answer, any answer that will explain life or maybe just the very moment you are in. You mindlessly roll a single grain of sand between your thumb and forefinger making half-hearted attempts to return to the moment where you are.

That's how I feel today on what has already started to be routine where I am at home on Mondays. I find myself almost dreading Mondays without work as much as when I did work.   I want to call my mother to ask how she handled her newfound freedom of retirement. She appeared to enjoy it. How did she pass the days?   What did she think about? She said she never looked back, she even moved from her family, not far, but far enough for a 90-minute car ride. Her retirement lasted four years. Her retirement ended before it really began. Is that how life is?

A colleague of mine said that she does not want to grow old. She said there is too much emphasis on the length of our lives (quantity) and not on the quality of the years. Not sure if I ever focused on the quality of life, it was just the life I lived, day-to-day. Life is and has been living one day followed by another.

28

Guilty—I'm already contemplating tomorrow when will I report to work. Ironically, once at work, I'll be thinking about what I will do the next free day. Go figure.

Where is that grain of sand? It kept me focused and held the universe.

The 1st Fourth

Remember tonight...
for it is the beginning of always.
Dante Alighieri

This will be the first Fourth of July (as an adult) that I will not be compensated by an employer. But now just about every other day of the week for me is like the Fourth of July. Freedom! Not being tethered to a 5-day workweek is enough to celebrate with fireworks. The Fourth is icing on the cake. So, what did I do on this unpaid holiday?

By now awakening at 7:30 in the morning had begun to feel natural. My dreams are uninterrupted, and this morning I *heard* in my dream Luciano

Pavarotti sing the well-known aria, "Vesti La Giubba" from Pagliacci. It is the scene where the husband dressed as a clown cries out that he has been the real fool. How strange, that twice this week I have dreamt of the late great tenor.

My husband turned around to face me in bed as if the music in my head awakened him. "Let's go out to breakfast," he immediately suggested.

Breakfast is my favorite meal whether I eat at home or out. "Can we afford it?" I ask.

"Of course," he assured me. Of course, what am I thinking. Breakfast is the least expensive meal to have out, and it is a leisurely way to start the day not to fuss in the kitchen. But first there's the cat box, their water bowl and food. Can't leave the house without first taking care of *our kids.*

At breakfast we discuss our plans for the day. We decide we'll take a walk right after we return home because the weather looks threatening. An unusual July 4th holiday with rain, I think. Clouds and wind, the temperature cooling down, the tail end of Hurricane Arthur is evident. My husband announces he will do some artwork which makes me happy because I need space to write. After our 2.5 mile walk he dives into his painting, leaving me to write.

Except—I just noticed those bathroom tiles really needed cleaning. In fact, the whole bathroom needed scrubbing. Our two cats track in hair and litter constantly every time they want to take a drink out of the tub. And would you look at all this dust. Forget about writing, my day is carved out with cleaning.

What is it about cleaning? It's minutia. But nothing could stop me. I just had to tackle the bathroom, today, right on July 4th! I was on a roll up to my elbows in scrub pads, vinegar and water, rags, paper towels, and sweat. Disgusting. That's it, that's what it is about cleaning. It's disgusting work. Geeze, and I'm not even getting paid for this today! It's all about satisfaction though and a sense of accomplishment. I don't know about you, but I don't feel accomplished after I clean the bathroom. I feel grateful that it's over.

Just before writing, I listen to "Vesti La Giubba" on YouTube. The tears run down my face uncontrollably.

It is a recording of Pavarotti's live performance in Munich back in 1986. Am I crying because Pavarotti is gone or because 1986 is gone? Gone are my thirties and when the world felt safer even if it was only an illusion. How could a day that started so spirited dissolve to a meltdown? I figured it out.

When you retire it is just as important to observe holidays as when it was a paid holiday off from work. Fortunately, the evening shaped out better. We went to see the fireworks display, something that we hadn't done for several years. It made me feel young, patriotic, my heart swelled with pride as I walked to the park seeing the next generation happy just as I was in my youth. A cool breeze was a welcome relief. Rain and humidity had vanished. Some spectators complained that the weather was too cool for July. For me it was a perfect summer evening.

Colorful illuminated wands held by children lit the park. As the dusk continued to grow to night, their flashing wands resembled fireflies. A side glance took me instantly to an earlier time when I spotted two young teenagers kissing against the fence. Her hair, long and brown, framed a pretty face. His face was hidden beneath a baseball cap but his developing muscular physique was prominently in view. So young, their love was urgent and as explosive as the eminent fireworks. Whereas my husband and I held hands, aware our spark was still there. It is an unhurried secure love that time spent together with the same mate brings.

The show kicks off with a recording of "Stars and Stripes, Forever" followed by Ray Charles' recording of "America the Beautiful."   One after another, gold, blue, and red streams of color each punctuate and illuminated the sky with successive booms.

The crowd cheered.

America, I love you.

When we returned home, I glanced at the Gerbera Daisy floating in the bowl, the one my husband gave me a few days earlier. It was still a bright magenta, still fresh.

Please tell me that is what it will mean to be retired.

Onward and Forward

If we fail to adapt, we fail to move forward.
John Wooden

This morning I awoke with an allergy attack. Couldn't stop sneezing and my nose was running like a stream. Still haven't gotten the hang of these three days at work and two days off because my off days have been filled with too much going on one day after the other. It's maddening.

Too many phone calls to make and follow-up. Gosh is this how retirement is spent, calling doctors, checking on paperwork, what ever happened to some fun in the afternoon. Some free time, riding a bike, strolling through the neighborhood, admiring a garden, seeing something of beauty. I'm not done with life by any stretch, but sometimes I think life is done with me.

Not so fast, I thought silently. An email from Literacy Volunteers arrived announcing an upcoming 6-week training workshop. The good news is that the workshops were all scheduled on one of my free days from work. I immediately respond and register for the training. Being a literacy volunteer is something I wanted for years but never had the time to pursue. I was instructed to gather materials at my local library to be prepared for the first session.

When I arrived at the library another idea surfaced. I always wanted to work in a library. Often I observed the ladies at the circulation desk and the ladies who shelved books and thought, "I could do that." I spontaneously inquired about any part-time positions and filled out an application. The supervisor said she had nothing yet but to call once a month to inquire. It would be months later when I was finally hired as a part-time Page at less than 12 hours each week.

Point to ponder: If you want structure during retirement it doesn't have to be another job. Accepting any employment could be going from the frying pan into the fire. For me, however, I went from the fire directly to soothing relief when I worked at the library.

If there is one take away from my retirement path is to choose carefully how to spend your time. By volunteering and the possibility of part-time library work, I felt confident to be on track toward a full retirement. Except for one word, worry.

Worry

Sufficient is the trouble for today.
Matthew 6:34

My cats sleep contentedly without a worry in the world as I write about my journey. Funny, they are part of it whether they know it or not. I must learn to live like a cat, only better. I think many people share this neurosis occasionally. The "worry syndrome" is more evident now than the past I think. Just surf the Internet to see all the global news that is fit to cringe. Worry is part of the 21st century human condition.

Let's be honest, when we were younger we believed retirement would be the end of worries, no more work, no more schedules and pressures.

Today's television ads further lull our generation into this mind trap depicting happy retired couples on perpetual vacations; dancing on the beach; and living in spotless houses. The awful truth is retirement brings a whole new set of stresses to each of us and advertisers know this. On any given day I receive mail and emails from companies about affordable life insurance; walk-in tubs; funeral expenses; new cures for back pain; cures for toenail fungus; and reverse mortgages.

Worry can be your new best companion in pre-and-post-retirement. But it doesn't nor should it be a constant one. Happiness and sadness live side-by-side throughout our lives. Recently I read that one of the biggest regrets older people have was they spent too much time worrying about things that never happened.

My cats only worry about their next meal or next cuddle, beyond that they are content with today. It will take a lot of inner-resolve and strength to conquer the worry syndrome, and it has been part of my path.

Friends & Boundaries

There is nothing on this earth to be prized than true friendship.
Thomas Aquinas

My friends call my mobile phone to chat on my days back at work because they have forgotten which days I'm home and which days I'm not. This brings me to a real concern. I love my friends, couldn't live without them, but a writer does need to write, and writing is a solitary activity. You may have an activity you have acquired since your retirement and want nothing more than to be immersed in its joy. That means little distractions such as early meet-up breakfasts, brunches, lunches, mid-afternoon teas, not to forget long phone calls, or Facebook. Besides with a skinny income and a bulging waistline, I can't afford to eat out too often.

One girlfriend said, "So now you're available to meet for coffee on Wednesdays." Another called and said, "I'm having a get together on a Wednesday in August, mark your calendar!" And another said, "We should walk more every week."

My husband is usually off on Wednesdays so that may cut into my time as well. How do I tell them that I'm getting my "sea-legs" at semi-retirement and may want some pajama days? What if I just want to meditate on the Gerbera Daisy? That I may want to do nothing or something alone or just be. How do I communicate that without hurting feelings?

A colleague of mine said I should not have told anyone that I am now home on what were once workdays. Well, maybe. But one of my friends will call my office phone, hear my new greeting, and wonder why I hadn't told her. I have even stooped to being vague which days I'm off. I feel like I'm not only undercover but have to take cover.

Friends are wonderful and an integral part of a healthy retirement plan and so is protecting your boundaries. Be not afraid to say, "No thank you," to the next luncheon invitation, set of tennis, Wednesday matinee, or teatime. It's your time, not anyone else's to dictate how you'll spend it.

Our time is finite. It took but a blink of my eyes to reach this age after sprinting through life, dashing to meetings, waking up early, writing down dates, and now do I really want to start filling my calendar with scheduled activities? What happened to winging it, spontaneity, rising in the morning and see how the day unfolds. Maybe it will lead to nothing but a satisfying day on the sofa, sipping tea, talking to my husband while we pet the cats. Is it a crime to do nothing? No, and nor is it a negative to plan events, to have something to look forward to.

I'm all for socializing and meeting with friends, but for me there is a genuine need to slow down, reflect, meditate, and relax. Now that you're retired don't let anyone make you feel as if you have to fill each day doing something. Social media posts will drag you into a scrolling abyss. The posts may make you feel as if everyone is having a lifetime of parties. Stop. Be choosey, choose to just be if you want, you have earned it.

Feel free to stretch out on the couch, grab a book, a magazine, close your eyes, dream, be still, and soak in the calm and tranquility of guilt free time.

Shedding My Former Self

*The privilege of a lifetime
is to become who you truly are.*
Carl Jung

What am I feeling today? Change is happening. My mind is whirling around in anticipation the way a child is fixated on her birthday party. For several years I've been daydreaming about semi-retirement, fearing that it may not be possible, and now that it is finally here I'm finding it almost impossible. What's wrong with me? Nothing.

I'm shedding. Like a butterfly breaking through its cocoon. Pieces of me are falling at my feet. There goes the calculator from work; the fixed smile to greet my colleagues has dissolved; the alarm settings on my mobile phone are deleted; the paid rubber stamp when tuition payments arrived locked away; the dressy black slacks moved to the back of the closet; one by one datum is eliminated from my memory just like HAL in Stanley Kubrick's film "2001."

There's a memory game that I play now and then. I think about the people whom I worked with over the decades. I imagine their faces, sometimes I recall their names to the forefront of my mind. Each time the game is played there is less recall, faces are indistinct. So many of my colleagues are now designated as Pat and Mary. I wonder whether they remember me.

It isn't an easy process. I'm a reluctant retiree. Not because I loved working or loved my jobs but I did recognize the important aspects of being employed fulltime.

I could walk confidently because I wasn't old yet. My job had become my shield against aging. I had a 9-5 job that locked me into the illusion of productivity, purpose, and dare I say, youth.

Does this sound familiar? Have you wanted to retire but hesitated because it crosses into a new frontier? You don't want to give up the paycheck, the status, the title, the bonuses, and identity, whatever it is. At this point it's all an illusion. You can't take any of that with you, you can't hold onto the illusion. The surrender may hurt. But retirement provides the opportunity to discover an identity that you may have ignored during your working years. Let go of the illusions, hold onto the memories, and then look forward. You will wonder why you ever hesitated.

Next chapter: Barbara from Florida shares what retirement means for her.

Barbara

Florida resident shares about her retirement.

I began working on my 16th birthday at Shop Rite in Teaneck, New Jersey. I was so happy to get the job because being part of the Baby Boomers meant you had lots of competition. In fact, I used a connection I had to get the job. My sister's boyfriend was already working there and recommended me for the position. I was thrilled that I would finally have some money to spend and save for a car, which was the ultimate symbol for freedom in those days.

After graduating college and becoming a certified public accountant, I entered the world of fulltime employment. At the age of 22 I land a post at one of the "Big 8" accounting firms and found myself as a young woman in a male dominated profession. I was a public accountant with numerous clients which meant I traveled all the while planning for my wedding!

A few years after the birth of my first son, I became a professor of accounting at a community college where I taught for 35 years. Of course, I knew that somewhere down the line I would retire but didn't really start thinking about it until I was in my 50's and only then because my husband is 3 years my senior. It always seemed so far away from the age I was.

I guess it wasn't until I reached 60 that I seriously started thinking more about it. I was looking forward to a pending retirement but was concerned about a few things: giving up my career (since there's no turning back); and had I planned sufficiently for my retirement (emotionally, financially, and socially) and whether I was ready for this abrupt change.

Though retired now for two years, I love it! I thought I might have some misgivings but so far, that's not the case. The benefits I enjoy are the freedom that being retired has given me, the freedom to sleep late and plan travel and activities during the week. A challenge I had anticipated is the amount of time that I am together with my spouse to the exclusion of most of the rest of the world. Working forced me to be out and interact with others. I would like him to be involved with his own activities and give me time in the home alone.

The Ground is Always Moving

For I know the plans I have for you,
plans to prosper you and not harm you,
plan to give you hope and a future.
Jeremiah 29:11

Security is a snapshot of an instant. The ground beneath my feet churns, rumbles and the image of an analog clock spinning minutes into weeks come to mind. Just when I thought I could settle into a routine and think that the retirement volcano will be dormant, an eruption has occurred. It was me, changing.

You may notice subtle signs of change but thought they would go away or hope circumstances would remain the same. We trick ourselves into not believing what we're feeling. This is what I must face now having made the decision to stop working full-time. Today the wind has left my sails. Emotionally the tide has risen over me. Hold on, hold on. I think Jeremiah 29:11.

The day started full of energy. Bright sunny morning had breakfast then went for a bike ride looking for something new in my own neighborhood. Looking for something different, something I haven't seen or experienced, except everything was familiar. I knew the route, the trimmed lawns and blooming gardens. Nothing new. I get it now. The ground is moving and will take me to where it wants. I'm not going to be grounded for a while. Yes, that's what I discovered today that I am faced once again with what to do with my life for the next 20 years. God willing.

It is similar to when your child goes off to college or moves out, you may struggle to redefine who you are and what you will do with more free time. You're not raising a child anymore, you're still a parent but it's different. Until you adjust to the inevitable change, you're paralyzed with fear of the unknown. You can go in numerous directions or stay planted in fear. This is where I am today, both restless and fearful. What's next? Tomorrow will be another day off from work. I will have to start thinking of it as another day to live. Keeping faith in one minute, one hour, one day. Tomorrow.

Ingmar Bergman Days

Everyone likes happiness, no one likes pain.
Ingmar Bergman

I was doing one of those retirement projects: organizing photographs. It was an archeological dig into my own past which surfaced forgotten memories both pleasant and less than. What followed was what my husband and I have dubbed "Ingmar Bergman Days."

Bergman, was an outstanding Swedish screen director, created films which delved into the dark side of life that often left me with an emotional hang-over. Unpacking recall is not always a good idea. But there I was doing exactly that.

It is true that some people belong to the world and so it is with Mother Theresa, Charlie Chaplin, Mahatma Gandhi, and Jackie Kennedy. Ingmar Bergman belongs to my world.

I became familiar with his films in my early 20s when I fell in love with foreign cinema. European films I found earthy, real, and focused on relationships, especially broken romances, and despair. Love and depression were an irresistible cocktail for melancholia.

My odyssey with Bergman started in the late 1970s while flipping through all of 13 TV channels. There on PBS was Bergman's "Virgin Spring" where the rape scene scared the beejeezus out of me. A glutton for punishment, I sat through "Seventh Seal";

was enchanted with his "Smiles of a Summer Night" "Monika" and of course, "Scenes from a Marriage." His work spoke to me.

Fast forward to 1999. Bergman Days started early into my dating with my husband to be. We were both haunted with regret about ex-spouses, just like Bergman characters. Fortunately for us we met at an age with gained insights. Together, we recollected through old photo albums, shared stories. We laughed and cried and consoled one another. It was around this time that we coined the phrase, *Ingmar Bergman Day*.

Most recently, the Ingmar cloud descended upon us when Steve's daughter married. Having gone through wedding ceremonies twice, we recognized the symptoms. We both had viewed "Scenes from a Marriage" with our first spouses. Here we were the day of his daughter's wedding and all our previous marital debris appeared. The age-old questions arose: How did the time pass so quickly? We had vowed once before to love, honor until death—what happened? Could it have worked? Was it my fault? Her fault? His?

Soul searching followed with bouts of tears and audible sobbing. Fortunately, this would not be a Bergman marathon. Sensibility prevailed. We praised the day, we prayed for Heather to have a happy wedding day and marriage. We survived, but still brought tissues to the church.

When Steve's son married, we were more in control and promised one another no Ingmar Bergman moments. All went well, that is until Steve saw his son at the altar. Emotions swelled. I glanced from the corner of my eye and saw tears rolling down Steve's face. I held his hand and wiped my eyes. Wedding ceremonies do exhume buried emotions.

Whenever we find one of us going down the wrong path, it is the job of the other to grab the other's hand and gently lead them to happier place. "No Ingmar" one of us will say. In a moment, sad thoughts are sent packing.

I know you'll be going through photos and cards when you retire. Just know it can hurt a bit.

Back at the Office

The more things change,
the more they remain the same
French proverb

Today I'll be back in the office and have already checked emails from home so I know what awaits me. Phone calls, return emails, Free Application for Federal Student Aid (FAFSA) verifications, and now I have a thesis to edit this week.

I don't want to go to work, I thought while having my breakfast fruit. That's not a good sign. Work is healthy, keeps us social, keeps our minds sharp, keeps money coming-in, food on the table, all that good stuff. I put on my fun summer outfit which is a colorful sheer vest I bought from Chico's, a silver-style bracelet my husband picked-up in Sugar Loaf, NY, and white top with white Capri slacks from Kohl's. Rested and refreshed from a morning shower, I felt good enough to walk on a model's runway.

Upon entering the office at 9 am I felt separate. Everyone was busy staring at their computers since 8 this morning. They looked like work-zombies. I was once a work-zombie, I still am except with one foot in retirement. The problem with going part-time on your former fulltime work is that you still think like a full-timer. I find myself thinking about the job, what to do the next day. What emails will be waiting, what fires will need to be extinguished, and I'm still in contact with all my colleagues which is not a negative.

Is the glass half-empty or half-full? It is both. When you're semi-retired make peace with it. Enjoy the day away because you have earned it; and remain conscientious when you return.

That being said, I am looking forward to a 3-day weekend which is just a day away. My glass will be full, maybe with wine.

Others May Resent Your Changes

She is clothed with strength…
she can laugh at the days to come.
Proverbs 31:25

The same colleague who called me on my first semi-retired day, called me at work today to ask me how is it working part-time? Did she expect me to say, "I hate it?" I mean what is to hate having an extra 24 hours of free time. She also added that I'm going to be "crazy busy" during enrollment periods and this is going to stress me.

I've already been stressed. Stressed working at 40-hours was too much.

Caught blind sighted, a realization flew into my face: Not only is it difficult for us to make changes, but others may find it difficult to accept the changes and may begin to question themselves.

Perhaps she is envious that I could go this route. I am 4 years her senior. But up until now, I have embraced work all my life. I have never been a slacker, always on time, always going the extra mile. In fact, I still do that even as a part-timer.

Is she looking out for my welfare? I don't know. Perhaps she thinks too many tasks at work with less hours to complete them will make me ill. I know this has happened to my husband. He and I have discussed that we can only do so much in one day because our stamina has lessened.

When my employer indicates I must leave, then I will jump off that bridge when I reach it. Until then, I am happy, gleeful even, to have two days off during the week, three-day weekends every week, sleeping in, walking by the Hudson River, having *elevensies*, and all the non-remunerated benefits that go along with semi-retirement.

Almost a Second Childhood

Age is never so old as youth would measure it.
Jack London

I feel like a kid on summer vacation! The day is spread out for me like peanut butter across Wonder Bread. Today is the day after what typically would have been a 3-day holiday weekend. Not for me this year. It is not only an extension of this holiday weekend, but it is my new normal. Every Monday I will be home. Holiday or not, Monday will be a day where I can decide what I want to do. That is, unless someone else has decided for me first. This morning my husband presented me with a list of galleries he would like me to query on his behalf. "Just three a week, don't feel pressured," he assures me.

Truth is media queries and pitches have been part of my "career" and his art. I'm a born advocate. I spend a good forty minutes looking up about six galleries, and only querying two. The other four were either closed or required an agent, or a phone call first which I wasn't keen on doing on a Monday morning.

This felt too familiar, like work. Not that I just want to play. In fact, a good citizen and good person of any pattern or color, would say that the right thing to do with additional free time is to help others. Not just your spouse, but your community, the nation, the world. I'm working on that and it will happen. In fact, I've taken it to a whole new level speaking to myself.

Be patient with me, I say to myself.

Okay.

Just don't go spend all your time in the shade ignoring responsibility.

Not a chance.

Okay, I'm watching you.

Shut up.

Now, to make some phone calls to let creditors know the schedule of revenue stream has changed. But first, a cup of tea is in order, and then a walk.

Beware of Retired Men

(Besides the one you may reside with.)

It's my day off and I am cooking as if I have eight arms. Stirring homemade vegetable soup; preparing bean salad with diced cucumbers and tomatoes, baking corn muffins; and cutting onions for a marinara sauce. I can't keep up with myself, how did I do it when I was working fulltime? Some women are fortunate to have husbands who share the cooking. My husband burns water. The cooking never bothered me; I love it. It is the constant meal planning and dishes from breakfast to lunch to dinner that I can't stand. This may be your situation when you and your husband are both retired.

You may leave the house for some needed space but you'll find retired men are everywhere. They are at the supermarket, the library, at the convenience store and they are armed with new pick-up lines. They come in every status and size, divorced, widowed, retired, never worked, and all appear to be looking for "M-r-s." that is, "Missing regular socializing."

One 80-something gentleman turned to me in the produce aisle to ask, "Is this an organic?" First, I thought he said "orgasm." He had a twinkle in his blue eyes and a ready smile. He had said what I heard. I guess a 62-year-old woman may look appealing to man of his age. I shrugged my shoulders and went back to my shopping. Another man ogled at my chest when I was searching through the mystery section at the library. I was wearing a modest top. His introduction was lame,

"Read any good books, lately?"

I smiled, grabbed the first flashy cover from the shelf and headed to the circulation desk.

It is loneliness; the need to connect that has prompted these encounters which breaks my spirit. Maybe I should have been friendlier—forget that. I have enough friends and my husband would not appreciate my keeping other men company.

Seriously, social contact is a challenge especially when singular. Friends and family have moved or are no longer ambulatory or passed away. I will be kinder and more mindful of this as I journey through retirement.

Meditation
Morning has broken, like the first morning…
Eleanor Farjeon - lyricist

Our bedroom windows face east and I've noticed how already the sun rises a little later each day and so do I. This morning I watch the sunrise and I ponder how this super star has been shining for millions of years all over the globe. Even more astounding is that this sunlight traveled for several million light years before it reached me. I don't know if this is an accurate figure, but it took a very long time. What does all this mean? I'm a late arrival on spaceship Earth, wandering through time, that is marked by calendar days, months, years.

There was a time when I would race out of bed to photograph the sunrises. Mostly during the winter when the sun came up later I would freeze in the pre-dawn air, waiting for a glimmer, a stream of light, first half-sun, then more, higher, brighter. Click. Photo taken. Trees in silhouette, red streaked clouds and then it was over as quickly as it arrived. Then I would rush to prepare for a day at work.

The first time I awoke for a sunrise was more than 30 years ago. Different bedroom where I stood over my daughter's crib watching in awe the transformation of the neighborhood while the summer sunlight bled across the sky. It was her first summer, like this is mine today. Retirement gives space and time to reflect.

Second Guessing

There are plenty of obstacles in your path.
Don't allow yourself to become one of them.
Ralph Marston

I had to switch my days this week so I'm still not quite into any groove. This is both frustrating as well as okay because this morning getting up and going to work on what would have been a day off, felt so natural. It made me ponder whether I am ready for this change of season. It didn't feel like summer to winter, but summer to autumn. Getting up early, making breakfast, showering, and dressing, preparing lunches, and out the door...easy, almost like riding a bicycle as the saying goes.

Funny thing is that several colleagues were shocked when I arrived at work. One was audacious enough to ask me, "Why aren't you out of the office?" It gave me pause before I even explained what I was doing there.

I'm second guessing myself and it's never too late for that when you are neurotic like me. But here I was thinking, "I could do this again, maybe all I wanted was a bunch of days off. Maybe all I really needed was a vacation. But have you ever felt after a lovely vacation that returning to work was like entering the gates of hell? We dread the emails, the phone calls, the faxes, the meetings. We almost don't care whether we do have a job waiting for us and that it is because of the job that has afforded us a vacation.

We're cranky, our internal clocks have gone awry, and we can't find anything to wear. All you may think of is "someday, I won't have to do this anymore. I'll be on a permanent vacation from work." Not…well maybe.

I am obviously blocking my own progress with too much overthinking. Definitely a pitfall when we have too little structured time.

In the next chapter, Sharon from New Jersey, shares her work and retirement path.

Sharon
*A New Jersey resident shares
about her career journey and subsequent retirement.*

After being a stay-at-home mom with my two sons for eight years, I felt compelled to get back into the world of work outside the home. Although, starting right out of high school, I had worked my way up through the ranks to executive assistant position at the New York Stock Exchange while taking college courses to achieve a BA degree, eight years out of the work force had me feeling insecure and inept and I began experiencing nightly dreams about applying for jobs and being rejected.

An ad in our local paper for an editorial assistant with a well-known textbook publisher caught my eye and seemed right for me since it was part time and ten minutes from my home. I applied and was thrilled to be offered the position on the spot, and I was beside myself with joy as I reported to my new desk every morning after dropping my boys off at school. Soon part-time became fulltime, and Editorial Assistant eventually became Managing Editor. Through the years, I'd think to myself, "I will never retire. I want to work until I die."

Early on, "the computer" was introduced to the departments in our company (each team had ONE computer that every team member shared). Then my electric typewriter was replaced by a laptop, then a desktop. (By then, every employee had her own.)

That was the beginning of the digital age and little did we know how immense the change would be.

Somewhere along the way through nearly three decades with this same company, and literally daily changes to workflow combined with the corporate mandate to work more with developing countries, and all while cutting back on staff, had me rethinking my "I will never retire" plan.

Soon after I entered my 60s, for several years I found myself thinking about the possibilities of retirement. My husband had retired recently, but that was no enticement to retire. Some of my friends were retiring from their jobs, but I still was very apprehensive about "not working." I think it was when the office began to feel like a graveyard: so many empty offices of people who had been downsized; the dead silence and stillness in the air; and the noticeable change in morale of the people who had survived the previous downsizings.

On March 21, 2014, I retired. The transition in seasons had me *spring* into action. I packed my remaining belongings and walked out of my office, down the stairs, out through the reception area, through the revolving door, and never looked back.

It's been more than four years since my retirement. I ask myself daily, "How did I ever manage to work and get everything done?" I am busier than ever, I feel. I am enjoying my life. I have found things I enjoy that I never even thought about doing before I retired. And I'm still finding new ideas, activities and, best of all, new friends.

I occasionally feel I'd like to have a job. Surely, I very much like the feeling of getting a paycheck. I sometimes think I will apply for a part-time job. But then I realize I'd have to give up the flexibility that I love in my days and weeks. I couldn't drop everything and run to take care of my grandchildren when my son or daughter-in-law find out at the last minute they need to work late, or go in early, or my grandchild is ill and can't stay at daycare. That's a "biggie!"

I was diagnosed with an immune-system disease several months after I retired. Although it didn't come as a complete surprise and I have not felt ill because of it, when it was confirmed, it did give me a feeling of additional justification for retiring at age 66 ½ (so young!).

My husband was diagnosed a year and a half ago with advanced stage of a disease that is often aggressive and fatal. That also gives one pause about the need to "work forever."

On the other hand, a close friend of mine told me yesterday that she was diagnosed with Stage 4 breast cancer and will undergo surgery and chemotherapy beginning next week. She has worked her entire adult life, while having a husband and three daughters at home. Mainly, she's run her own businesses, so she has some flexibility, but also is motivated to work exceptionally long hours, often seven days a week. She told me she will try to find people to fill in for her and help out, but she cannot allow herself to abandon her two partners with the new business they started a year ago. She is close to 80 years old. May her energy hold out and her amazing attitude carry her through.

All in all, I love retirement. Most important is that everyone should have the *option to retire* when she so chooses.

The Library – Oh Joy!

*I always thought that paradise
will be a kind of library.*
Jorge Luis Borges

The Pearl River Public Library has been my home away from home for more than 15 years. The staff is friendly, the patrons friendly, reference librarians helpful, the environment is clean, orderly, quiet, and holds a collection of books which encompasses every subject imaginable. Of course I wanted to work there, belong to this team. I was born to work at a library only I took the long route to reach it.

At the interview I was asked whether I could stand on my feet for 3-4 hours. I've been standing on them for 8 hours at the college job because I opted for a standing workstation. Yes, I can stand for 3-4 hours. You'll have to stretch, bend, sometimes carry books, walk around the library, push in chairs, keep things orderly, and shelf-read.

So the above is in a nutshell what a Library Page does. And here is what I don't do:

No e-mail, no phone calls, no computer work, no maintaining databases. Sounds like a piece of heaven to me. I was hired!

Oh dear, now I have two part-time jobs.

Hello New Pain

Be content with an ordinary life.
Laozi

Today I awoke with an unfamiliar ache. Isn't the human body remarkable that it reminds us almost daily that we are aging? I say to it, "Hello new pain." It replied with a twinge stretching across my left shoulder.

Fortunately, it is a day that I am not at work and can nurture my being. A hot shower makes it feel much better. Next on the menu was a fresh cup of coffee, a soft straight-back chair where I ease into, two aspirin, sip the brew, and look outside. I see a bird in flight and the sun is breaking through several dark clouds.   This is so much better. Better than what?

Better than root canal, better than having to go to work with this pain, better than many ailments I do not allow my mind to visit.   So, on this day I count my blessings and because of this unexpected painful visitor I appreciate an ordinary day at home.

Interlude

What a sweet delight a quiet life affords.
Henry Drummond

Today is a Sunday. Most Sundays I have been exhausted from running around the previous day in attempt to complete all the errands that I had no time for during the workweek. Sound familiar? Now with the newly found luxury of having Mondays free I am not feeling as pressured. Life's pace has gone down a notch.

And what other perks are associated with retirement besides more time? Saving on gas, your wardrobe stretches out into weeks; you can sleep-in for 40-minutes and not worry about arriving to work late; a second cup of tea at 9:30 feels so natural and gives me time to pause and reflect; I see my neighbors a little more; I feel connected to the community more; there's time for writing and collages; I have time to enjoy a quiet day. I am not rich in the material sense but I have all that I need right this very moment in time. Isn't that what rich is all about? How is it possible that 24-hours can create such a different perspective on being? It is nothing short of a miracle.

What is Retirement?

Retirement is…

This may strike you as strange that I ask this question amid the journey, but one never knows what something will be until they are involved with it.

Psst, I'm going to let you pre-retirees in on a big secret that the Department of Labor or Motley Fool will not tell you: Retirement is FUN! F-U-N. It's not what it is, it's what you and the good Lord make it. Isn't that how it has been for every aspect of living up until now? Some of you may say, big deal, this lady has a part-time job. It is a big deal for this woman to work part-time, collect social security and enjoy free time. Besides, retirement is not just a state of being. It is a state of mind, an unstressed mind.

Life milestones are many in any woman's life with or without marriage and children. But speaking from my limited perspective I clearly see the milestones in my life that may sound familiar such as, college, marriage, childbirth, and parenthood; career launch, parents passing, divorce, remarriage, menopause; semi-retirement, retirement; friends moving, and death of a partner.

How well we handle these life changing events is critical to our emotional and physical health, and especially when our lives are less structured with fulltime employment. Some of the things already discussed are ways to help you cope. For me, I have maintained friendships, exercised with walking and bicycling, enrolled in continuing education courses, held family gatherings, volunteered, worked part-time, and continued to write.

ElderChicks.com is a web site that I came across after reading the bloggers' book, "The New Senior Women" by Barbara M. Fleisher and Thelma Reese. Women across the country were interviewed about how they handled one of the major milestones in most people's life, but specifically women near or past retirement age and beyond. What surprised me most were the women who engaged in a second career.

What exactly is this thing called retirement? Surely one cannot be retired from life. It's not as if a person leaves a fulltime job, goes home and rolls-up into a ball waiting for God. And that was the exciting aspect of the book and the blog, how women allowed their inner compasses to roam freely.

They discovered new interests, friends, talents, and in the process some launched a business; others became advocates for social issues; they took classes or even went on to complete a college degree; and yes, second careers. Echoed throughout is how each of these women grappled with change in the season in our lives.

Today I am feeling the empowerment of being untethered to my cubicle. I can look out to the horizon and see an exciting day ahead, perhaps many days ahead. That is what retirement does, it

lets us see. We are past the walls of brick and mortar
that enclosed us, past counting the clock. Aren't we?

Me in We

The best thing to hold onto is each other.
Audrey Hepburn

How special one free day can be! An ordinary day filled with special moments. It called to me the moment I awoke. The sky was filled with puffy white clouds and abundant sunshine. We (my husband and I) decided to play tennis after I wrote and after he worked on his art followed by a quick snack and then to the tennis courts. Not a soul on the courts, hitting back and forth, laughing at one another like a couple of kids. Not every day will be like this but today we said no schedule, no pressure, nothing on our calendar except the two of us and whatever we decided to do.

Later we walked along the jetty in Piermont, sat by the river dreaming, I took a couple of photos, we looked at rocks and sticks, the scent and sight of wildflowers filled our senses. Still not ready to go home yet, we decided to browse through a store with hundreds of gift items for the home, odd and unusual, cheap, and expensive. We consumed all the visual beauty, garish, and whimsical, bought nothing. We were filled to the brim with happiness.

Not every retiree is part of a couple, so what I do say to those that are is cherish the moments you do have together. It may have taken you both a lifetime to reach this point. Rediscover your partner in ways that may surprise both of you. Your partner may want to cook meals together; or read a book with you and discuss it; go to poetry readings; grow a vegetable garden; or simply sit with you quietly holding your hand.

Just as work and careers have come to an end, the sun will set each day. Today was truly a gift. Fell asleep without a care on my mind. Not really, tomorrow I would be back at work.

Making New Friends

The only way to have a friend is to be one.
Ralph Waldo Emerson

Today is my free Monday, already cluttered with "to do" items. The one bright spot is meeting a new friend for coffee this morning. I would never have thought of making a new friend at this point in my life, but there is something very special about Lola. She is an acquaintance I have held at arm's length while we worked together, yet a friendship was developing. What makes her special though is that I have unconsciously not had people of color in my life until now. What does this have to do with retirement? I'm glad you asked.

Retirement is freeing which allows us to explore all the possibilities in our lives. Well, not those that may be harmful to us or others, but possibilities within reasonable limits. Making friends and especially new and younger friends is an imperative as we age. Our established friends may move far away, become ill, or even die.

When I was a child I learned a little jingle as a Brownie, "Make new friends, and keep the old. One is silver the other gold." Today Lola is silver but years from now, I may consider her a golden friend.

I arrived early at our planned meeting place. A spacious self-serve café not linked to any national chain. I chose the perfect table facing the front window so I would see Lola as soon as she arrived.

There I waited excited for myself to have made this step toward a new friendship, and excited because I hadn't seen Lola for two months since the college dismissed her. And I waited.

The cashier noticed me, I was sure he was thinking: *What is this lady doing just sitting here and not ordering anything?* I tried to busy myself looking through my purse, checked phone messages, and waited more for Lola's arrival. It was now almost 25 minutes past our agreed meeting time. Always the optimist, I went to the counter and paid for two coffees and two egg-cheese sandwiches and returned to the table. My mobile phone sounded. It was Lola. *Sorry, Joan, I'm running late but I'm on my way!* At last, she arrived. We laughed and talked for about two hours.

Before bed I thought how today, a gorgeous mid-summer day, was filled with endless possibilities. Still, I ask myself that nagging question "What have I accomplished today?"

Unlike the office where papers in the outbox can be counted, or the number of tests corrected if you're a teacher, or the number of customers you may have serviced at a bank, retirement days can't be measured or quantified. The accomplishment mindset is a treadmill and pitfall that may be difficult to release. Think quality.

I thought of something Lola said just before leaving,

"I hope we keep in touch."

I smile and fall asleep.

From the Heart

Write them on the tablet of your heart.
Proverbs 7:3

"Your first draft you write with your heart; your second draft you write with your brain." These words so impressed me from the movie *Finding Forrester* as a writer. The reclusive famous older author mentors the young, gifted student and guides him to life's direction. The author in turn changes the course of his life before it is too late.

I have noticed that many activities not just writing we do first with our hearts and later with our brains.

Am I feeling regrets about semi-retirement? Was this a heart blunder and brainless pursuit?

The journey did begin with a splash of giddiness and heartfelt joy on the prospect of not reporting to the same old grind each day of the 5-day workweek. That was my first draft. Now, for the rewrite.

My mind reasons that retirement is a constant tweaking and rewriting of the plot, the characters, the dialogue, and especially the main character (you) of the story. Your story. What will your retirement turn out to be?

There are no musts or rules about retirement, and that's what makes it both exciting and daunting. We set our rules, and the help of spiritual guidance. Was reading a passage from Paramahansa Yogananda's about success and he states that our journey in life is to find God. So, it's not to be God, not to say that we are solely the master of our lives. That is what I am also finding out with retirement. You plan and then other variables will emerge which are not under your control. Live with an open heart (your draft) and an open mind (your brain) to opportunities and possibilities.

On the next page, you'll read how, Joy Shaw, transplanted from New Jersey to Pennsylvania has kept her mind and heart open in the face of life changes.

Joy Shaw

Pennsylvania resident and recent widow shared her employment journey and retirement path which created enduring lifetime friendships and strong faith.

I started working after completing two years of secretarial college. My first employment was at a small financial firm as Secretary to the VP. Working fulltime outside the home when I started a family wasn't possible. My daughters were little and my oldest daughter was ill, but I did temp work whenever I could.

I started part-time at an agency in Ridgewood (Walker Personnel) that offered typing services (yes, still on electric "manual" typewriters), got my personnel license, and have thought about writing a memoir about those experiences titled "Temporarily Yours."

From there, in 1985, I placed myself with Crew Engineers as Office Manager and stayed there for 31 years. They were my Crew family. We saw one another through corporate and personal turbulence, and we all remained intact and stronger for it. I never really thought about retiring as I loved my job so much and knew financially it was wise to work so long as possible.

I loved the challenges of learning new computer programs as they evolved and, for the most part, was the only "show in town" to run an engineering office. I retired in December of 2016 to care for my husband Wesley. This was not a difficult decision as he needed me, and financially it didn't make sense to pay aides and daycare more than I was earning. I was not upset, just did what needed to be done. Wes ultimately had to be placed in a facility; the house in NJ had to be sold; I moved to Pennsylvania to be nearer to family, hoping to find a facility nearby for Wes. He passed away before that could happen and here I am.

I miss working and having a purpose, but God has placed me here and I am grateful. Having two major surgeries this past year, family nearby has meant so much, and now my daughter may need me after her heart bypass surgery. God has always led me on the right path. I live in a 55+ community and enjoy hearing stories from those neighbors who are still working and those retired.

There's a lot of loneliness to contend with, so I try to visit and help those who can no longer drive. I've met new friends through a knitting group and chair yoga at the library. I knit for charities and that has given me purpose. I am grateful to still be in touch with my Crew family and my New Jersey friends through social media and still able to drive to see them. It's not easy to reinvent yourself in a new place as a retired widow, but God is good and leads the way and gives me strength.

Is Your Age Showing?

*Age is simply the number of years
the world has been enjoying you.* Unknown

It's funny how others will quickly attribute retirement and age to forgetfulness or slip-ups. Retirement does not mean dumb, forgetful, senile, past your sell-by date, out of the loop, or looped. It doesn't even mean retired especially if you decide like I did to have a part-time job. But just let one mistake happen, or funny incident where your *age* may be called into question and colleagues will POUNCE at the chance to razz you. And so today I had a taste of that.

The incident was my addressing our VP of the college by an incorrect first name, twice. Once when I greeted him, and just before he left our office. One of my office mates questioned why I called him by that first name. I assumed she meant that I shouldn't be addressing our VP by his first name. I replied, "I can address him by his first name Richard if I want." To which all of them replied, "But his name is Robert!"

"Senior moment, Joan!" Followed by peals of laughter. It was a funny moment that even I laughed. But somewhere down deep it hurt and it shouldn't have. It made me reflect when I have done that to others.

Here's a memory. I recall a silly laugh at my mom years ago when she kept watering a silk rose and was amazed how it never died. But I never thought for one moment it was because she was getting older. But what about times when we have made assumptions about people based on the color of their skin, their last name, their sexual orientation, or age?

Semi-retirement has taught me two lessons: not to make quick assumptions because someone has gray hair and not to take myself too seriously. I will continue to laugh at myself as I always have and not so quickly laugh at others.

A New Groove

I'm retired, I do whatever I want. Anonymous

The weekend can be just as challenging as the weekdays that you have off. How are Saturdays and Sundays different than when you may have lived for the weekend, shouted TGIF, the hump-day Wednesdays, the Good Lord it's Mondays? Did you know that the most neglected day of the week is Tuesday? And it shouldn't be because people are probably more productive on Tuesdays once they're back into the 5-day workweek routine.

Now in a new groove arrived great expectations. The garage is finally going to be tackled. The photos will be organized; drawers will be neater; cupboards cleaner. Forgettabout it! A spotless house may be a sign of lack of focus on important life concerns. I am not proposing to live in chaos. That is an unstated understanding. What I advocate for myself and you, yes **you**, is to get out of the house and do something else.

My first breakout weekend began in mid-May. I slept-in an extra 30-minutes instead of worrying if I'll have enough time to finish the usual Saturday errands. This was a baby-step followed by a giant step. After breakfast and a shower, I went for a bicycle ride, not far, just five miles. The exercise and additional sleep set the day into high energy. I didn't feel like I was treading along the usual Saturday hamster-wheel.

I greeted and chatted with my neighbors when I returned the bike back to the storage room. Had a second cup of tea and read the paper, every page except the obituaries.

Ordinary you may say, yet small changes can make you feel extraordinary and empowered. You don't have to leap from a plane right after you retire to breakout of your routine. Walk, read, take a class, garden, meet a friend for breakfast, call your local volunteer office and see what's needed in the community. Oh, and yes, you can choose to do nothing, but don't turn it into a marathon of nothing where your days stretch to an empty array.

Back to weekends, there is the temptation to do what you always did on weekends. You know the drill: errands, laundry, food-shopping, cleaning. I suppose conventional wisdom tells us not to take too much of a departure from the familiar, and that may be because we cling to it like secure safety net. Just the way we cling to our jobs.

I dare you this Saturday or Sunday to do something that you wouldn't normally do but have longed to do. Those little 48 hours don't have to be thought of as 'the weekend." They are now part of your days as they always were, it is a state of mind not only a state of being. It is what your *retirement* can be.

Charlotte, a Massachusetts resident, shares her work and retirement journey next.

Charlotte

*Massachusetts resident, formerly
from the UK and Australia*

I need to point out, in the town where I resided in Australia, there was 16K population and it was the largest town for **600** miles. There was little in the way of real work for women except nursing. (Teaching required going to college and none of our teachers were locals). But at the legal age 15 in Oz, there were job opportunities at the local and the **only** large chain general merchandise store.

I don't remember how I felt the first time I heard, "You're hired." But I do recall I would come home almost in tears from my feet aching, but soon adjusted and loved having the money and what that made possible, such as clothes, makeup, etc.

My longest employer stretch was about 9-10 years and there are three of them, with that length of time. I was a career changer, first as a professional draper for the New York Metropolitan Opera, then a 10-year stint at a marketing firm; and later I earned a Master's degree in computer science and worked as technical support traveling to various places within the Continental United States.

I guess about age 55, after I felt I could no longer endure the required traveling, I started to think about retirement. My job essentially vanished with the financial crisis four years later, so I worked up a retirement plan and decided I could probably manage with part-time work and the savings I had.

When I began to think about retirement I was anxious but reasonably confident my retirement plan was solid. The financial crisis put a dent in my confidence but as I probably would not have been able to find commensurate work. I just had to deal with my emotions, after all it was anxious time for everyone, my concerns paled by comparison.

Now that I am fully immersed in retirement for more than 5 years, I stay remarkably busy, and enjoy the 'work' part of it, as there is no stress, and it is diverse and optional. For me, the challenge is in being self-motivated and recognizing just how much time must be allocated to activities that keep us healthy.

Mondays

Good Lord It's Monday – Anonymous

In the course of your working life you will report to a job for at least 2,085 Mondays. That is 5 years and 7 months of Mondays where you asked colleagues how their weekends were. That is a lot of time devoted to ask others how their weekend was especially when you can barely remember what you did those 48 hours. However, there is an unspoken understanding that you are in these Mondays together. It's a badge of honor to be grumpy on Monday mornings. It is expected, accepted, and respected.

These past few Mondays I gaze outside my kitchen window at the cars whizzing back and forth during rush hour. I used to be one of them. But now as a part-time employee my *Monday* is Tuesday.

So when I arrive on Tuesday morning, my colleagues had bonded through Monday, there's a hint of frost in the air as if to say, "Humph, here she comes strolling in on Tuesday, and she'll be off tomorrow. What a deal." It is a deal, and I have worked for it and didn't know how long it will last.

Here's a tip for those of you who are considering working part-time at your current situation or with a new employer: request Mondays as one of your free days. It tacks on nicely to your Friday evening, Saturday, and Sunday. Mondays are not that important in the whole scheme of things. Some of the worst work mistakes are made on Mondays. I recall one boss who always scheduled office meetings first thing Monday mornings. It set the mood for the entire week, and not in a positive way. I was younger then, born in a different era which accepted it unquestioning.

Take Your Time

*Enjoy yourself,
it's later than you think* – old tune

A week whizzed-by and I didn't write one word! How could I be so busy not to think of writing? What could have taken my time to not provide even 20-minutes to sit down and write something, anything. What about you? Are there things that you love to do but you find yourself keeping busy with day-to-day chores? We're like hamsters spinning in an endless wheel, going faster and faster and still in the same place. What is exactly wrong with that? What is wrong with simply living one's life day-to-day? Time-management gurus, retirement counselors, and life coaches will tell you to plan, have a goal, keep moving, be productive, be social, and oh yeah, relax! Their advice is based on the "doing model" and just "to be."

All this advice makes me feel guilty and confused. I'm constantly monitoring myself. Am I being a slug too often? What have I accomplished today besides living the past 24-hours? All I know is that I don't want my life to pass without meaning, without love for others, without helping others.

Live Simply

Life is really simple, but we insist
on making it complicated.
Confucius

Do you remember that song by Bobby McFerrin, "Don't Worry, Be Happy?"

It was the joke around an editorial office when we were stressed about deadlines; it was the song hummed while standing in line at the supermarket; it was the tune played frequently on the radio; and for some it nearly became a mantra, an attitude, a philosophy. Then some smart-ass retaliated with "Don't worry, life crappy." That is closer to what a lot of retirees may be feeling.

Last night on Frontline they featured the "Retirement Gamble" and explained how Wall Street is robbing workers of their 401K retirement money through hidden fees and is tantamount to gambling. I personally know several people who never purchased stock, never joined a 401K. and are more solvent than those who have. I'm not one of them. Financial solvency has avoided me most of my life.

Many of those interviewed for the PBS documentary expressed concern, lamented that they may have to work all their lives, have lost a lot of money with the dot.com bubble bursting, while sitting in comfortable though modest homes. They all looked well fed, wore nice clothes, were not ill, had their freedom, one even rode a motorcycle. I have a friend who retired six years prior to me. She lives in a lovely home surrounded by an expansive yard and garden, stayed at the same company for 20+ years, her husband is a retired professional, and yet she has more than once said, "I worry about money." Yet another friend jokes that the beauty of not having much is that you don't have to worry about losing much.

What does it take to simply be happy in retirement? Does it take a million dollars? Living the touted "good" life? Most will say if they're able to keep their home, go on a special vacation, see friends and family, and enjoy relatively good health, this would be a fulfilled retirement. Retirement happiness is simply to live and to live simply.

What is New?

There is nothing new under the sun.
Ecclesiastes

I found myself staring mindlessly at one of those 24-7 news channels. It was one of my free days while holding my thoughts in bondage. Nothing was new. The world is crashing with wars, murders, protests, civil unrest, police brutality, torture, human trafficking, drugs and more. It was otherwise a decent weather day but it looked bleak from the window of my computer and television screen. I was grateful when my phone rang to interrupt this barrage of everything I didn't need to know.

When you're retired you have the spare time to access all the bad news enough for a lifetime thrown at you in the span of just minutes. It can be difficult to turn your attention away from the headlines and leave what is best left unknown. This doesn't mean hiding beneath the bed covers but instead sifting through the ruckus to catch the gentle call of a songbird that may otherwise have gone unnoticed under the pounding sound waves of negative news. The agreeable weather and a walk nearly escaped me today.

If we agree that we cannot know everything, cannot do everything, experience everything in one lifetime, maybe even a hundred lifetimes, what purpose does it serve to fill our minds with bits of tragic news that may be happening across the globe?

Okay, I already hear many of you saying, "Well, do something about it." What can be done? Write a check, pray fiercely every day, join a peaceful protest, join an organization that shares your concerns.

Another way is to keep your mind strong, stand guard at what you allow to pass through the gates of your consciousness. It begins with taking care of ourselves first. If you by now have a new daily routine of waking at a reasonable time (not too late), walking, eating less sugar, and drinking water, you are already on the path to making yourself insulated. You'll have the energy to move away from the computer and television, and away from those scary headlines.

Certainly, retirement is about change, about concern for humanity, not just our own survival. Begin with yourself, make yourself strong, healthy, pleasant, peaceful, and then tackle the wounds of the world from strength. You'll find in the process that this will improve your days providing purpose to your retirement.

Will you choose to fill your head with negative information day-after-day until you're afraid to do anything? There may be nothing new under the sun, but this is your first new retirement.

Forgotten Facets

*When will you begin that
long journey into yourself?*
Rumi

Is there an activity that makes you feel young, rejuvenated. I feel slim on the tennis court even with the extra 10 pounds. I can still run around the tennis court like I'm forty-something. Except after 30-minutes of intense play my face becomes fire-engine red, my head is dripping in perspiration and all the balls start staying on my side of the net.

Even so, the encouraging aspect is that I can still play, still run, laugh at myself and my opponent, and for a half hour cares of the world vanished. The focus is simply on the ball, the net, and the racquet. You can have a living in the moment experience or not, for me the newfound love of tennis only happened after retirement.

There is probably something you enjoyed doing but haven't attempted in perhaps decades. I know a woman who joined a ballet class. It made her happy and sad all at once because it was her mother who bought her first tutu and ballet slippers. It was my parents who purchased my first tennis racquet with green stamps. Does anyone remember green stamps?

One Saturday my folks gathered all their stamped-filled books, drove to the redemption store and I chose my first racquet. I was thrilled. It started a lifetime enjoyment of the sport which sadly was abandoned for 25 years. Now in my sixties I'm back on court and it feels wonderful. I found a part of myself that I didn't realize I was missing. Truthfully, I don't play every week or even every month. Frequency has never been my strength. The strength is having the time to choose when to play.

What facets of yourself have you forgotten? Leisure time is on your side. Once retired you may rediscover activities you once enjoyed.

The Words Gave Me Pause

The Lord gives and the Lord takes away.
Job 1:21

I have arrived at an age where there is time to join a book club. How wonderful it was to find a group of women who share the joy of reading and discussion of what they read. One book we just read was Alice Hoffman's "The Dovekeepers." Hoffman's words "...what has been given can also be taken away," caused me to pause. This was not a new idea or nothing that I haven't thought of or perhaps even said myself, but to see it in print coming from a character of the first century caused a strange uneasiness within me.

We have surpassed the first century living, yet we remain in human frailty.

Here I am enjoying semi-retirement for all of two months and suddenly I am frightened how quickly it all can end. Not my life, but how the circumstances could come to a halt without notice. What kept the Dovekeepers grounded and hopeful, was their faith. I wish that is all it would take for me to stay grounded and hopeful is to have faith in God. We witness it every day on the news. People lose their homes in a fire; loved ones at war; car crashes; earthquakes, and they still speak with words of grace that they have survived to rebuild their lives. Survival it seems is all that matters, not how one will live after the survival, but to be alive.

To be alive is a gift and blessing, and I do cherish my first summer in a new season of life. I will do more than survive. I will charter the days with my journal, and I will live. I will not be afraid of what I have no control. To persevere in the face of struggles must be what faith is. Tucked in the back of my mind is what has been given may be taken away.

I refuse to relinquish my retirement. In the next chapter you'll read it all may be an illusion.

You Can't Retire from Life

*Flow, flow, flow.
The current of life is ever onward…*
Kobodaishi

It will not matter if you reside in your own home or an apartment. (I am an apartment dweller.) There are monthly bills, taxes to pay, events to attend, family dinners to prepare, chores. Regardless of your employment status, life is work. True, luncheons, matinees, and sitting on the sofa reading a book are part of retirement. But to think "someday when I'm retired…" will be some sort of Utopia is unrealistic. Well, I wish someone had told me that. We women have a built in "do machine" that is difficult to turn off.

We must do that report; we must do something to feel productive; must write that "to do" list.

There has been a flurry of freelance work these past two weeks. The problem with freelance work when you're retired is it reminds you that you're still working.

Tonight, when I went to bed I was thinking about the article to write, a phone interview, and did I spell everyone's name correctly? There were two lists on my nightstand. One listed the mundane laundry, food items to be purchased, and whether I should invite my friends for a Friday night supper. The other list had names, emails, and phone numbers of people I was chasing for a quote and information for my freelance assignment.

Apartment life has its benefits and pitfalls. But I hear the angst my homeowner friends express about broken appliances, the need for a new roof, increased tax assessments, and yard upkeep. It's about the money.

Those are not my worries as a tenant. The obvious pitfall is no equity growing and having enough money to live. That is why I am semi-retired. It's about the money.

Give Yourself Permission for Solitude

To understand the world,
one has to turn away from it on occasion.
Albert Camus

Today I have turned off my phone. I know that's not a big deal, but for me it makes me feel ashamed. What if a friend calls and I choose to ignore her call. Stop. I must remind myself that I am semi-retired and want to do somethings that I have been unable to do while working five days each week. Last week I was nailed to the phone when a coworker called to chat. I wouldn't have mind a little break from my writing, but it turned into a 40-minute filibuster about the office!

I have acquired good friends along the way as I wandered through various careers. I say various because at the heart of it all, I am a writer, not the PR Director, the substitute teacher, the assistant editor, or the financial aid counselor, the position that I continue to work at now.

As time goes forward, sometimes these alliances that we made along the way don't last. This is not to say that we have used people or have been used, it's just a fact of life that as we live, we evolve and sometimes we don't want or need another new gal pal, and especially one who was basically an office friend. Does this sound heartless?

I have had more than my share of one-time lunch dates, dinner with the girls, an afternoon coffee, or simply a long-winded phone conversation that struck me as going nowhere and a complete waste of time.

At this point in our lives we know who our friends are and we hold them dear. The new friends we may make will probably share an interest of ours. Until our paths cross, I'll keep my own company and the company of those I've known for years.

Younger Generation

Youth has no age.
Pablo Picasso

What can the younger generation teach us now that we're older wiser know-it-alls? As it turns out, quite a bit.

Lately, I often ask my thirty-something daughter for her input on my writing as she and I share this endeavor. It is our destiny. What surprised me is how she is surprised by the fact that not only do I accept her guidance, but I welcome it.

Years ago, when she was a teen, she would have fought me on any advice. Then she entered her twenties and started to not only ask for my opinion but thanked me for it as well! The tables have turned. She holds the keys to the future, and I am keeper of the past who tries extremely hard to stay up to date with her and the rest of the world.

You may be blessed with grandchildren, the very youngest of generations who speed through rooms while expressing pure bliss with yelps and giggles. If you're fortunate you may be able to hug them for a few minutes, get a messy kiss and catch the scent of their youth. Oh to be little again without a care! In the same moment you feel the pang of passing time you can be on the floor playing, acting silly, laughing until your sides hurt, and erasing all signs of age.

All this affirms for me how important it is for us to remain open to new voices, even the wee ones. Is there a young adult, a teen, or child who wants to share information with you—my advice is to listen. Someday they may even be curious what it was like for you years ago.

Pets

Time spent with cats is never wasted.
Sigmund Freud

This past week I came upon two articles which sung the praises of owning a pet. We have two cats, Mango and Coco. We love them…most of the time. Each day for ten years, my husband and I went off to work and before closing the door would say to our cats, "You be good boys." Each day after work, there they were sitting together at the kitchen window waiting for our return. God only knew what our two cats did after we left. Now retired, I know.

Fast forward to this summer when I started staying home for two days each week. The bigger guy,

Mango, stared at me constantly waiting for treats, extra food, extra lovies, turning on the water in the bathtub for him. I had become his slave in a matter of days. And his smaller litter mate, Coco, would constantly meow in my face for his share of attention as well. If I went to the bedroom and closed the door, I could hear them pawing the door for entry. It was no use. It was obvious I have retired for their benefit. What can't I understand about that?

If you don't already have a pet dog or cat, retirement is an excellent time to adopt one. That is if you're ok with being tethered to their needs. Consider if this responsibility is what you want with your new retirement. Personally, I reveled in the company of our two cats.

The home front eventually calmed down. They adjusted to my new schedule and they know that I still rule the roost. Like the articles I read, pets are part of the family and they know it. Now I know it. Freud knew it.

Transformation is a Continuum

I am a verb.
Buckminster Fuller

A colleague of mine who is at least 20 years my junior was recently let go from her position. She had a very prominent post and did a remarkable work for the past 19 years. Change. There's that word again. Our place of business saw a new vision, new possibilities and somehow this reliable, intelligent, personable woman was not part of the new view or landscape.

A light bulb went off. She is not going to retire, but she has been faced with change just as I have. The process of reevaluation, regrouping, reinventing, digging deep within and asking difficult questions of herself; just as I have and continue to do.

Do we ever stop? Plato said, "an unexamined life is not worth living." This thing we call "retirement" is just part of a continuum we all know as life. It stretches beyond the horizon where we can't see. Sometimes there are no signs, and no directions to give us an idea of what will await us. Our journeys are not exactly under blindfold, but a lot requires faith.

My colleague is destined for better positions than the one she lost this past week. She will begin the process of career evolution, hopefully not too often. By the time she reaches my age, she will recognize change as an inevitable process.

Which brings me to this thought. Leading toward retirement is a process of change, and once retired we will continue to evolve. There are remarkable individuals who choose to work into their 80s and even 90s. The operative words are the "freedom to choose."

Gratitude

Just to be is a blessing.
Just to live is holy.
Abraham Herschel

I entered a blog post on Elder Chicks and it was published and received comments! It thrilled me. My goal is to eventually make mention of my writing and my books, treading slowly. Their web site is well put together and draws information and blog postings from many different women. I'm not sure if they would consider me an "elder chick" at 62, but I'm getting there and feeling the same growing pains they may have. Fortunately, this is a resource for women who move from the employment to retirement, even if it is semi-retirement as mine.

Speaking of which, today I spent my day off truly the way I had envisioned it when I thought about working part-time. I didn't rush my breakfast, chatted with my husband, even had a second cup of tea. Went food-shopping before he left for work, then sat down and wrote the first 2,100 words of my cozy mystery, *Tea & Deceit.* I was able to fit in a walk, and then return home and make a delicious *ratatouille* for dinner, and homemade vegetable soup for Saturday when my daughter visits. This has been a wonderful day and it isn't over yet. Tonight, I am attending a free workshop on memoir writing at a local library.

I've met all my monthly bills, though I am bummed that I don't have much disposable cash. Yet, I am incredibly grateful for the money and that I am still able to carry on with my humble lifestyle. I know there are people my age fully retired, traveling, vacationing, buying items for their home, having lavish dinners...but I also know there are people who have much less than I who would trade places with me in a heartbeat.

Volunteer

It is when you give of yourself that you truly give.
Kahlil Gibran

I want to give back. My volunteer work teaching English would impact the future and the future of American generations. I tutored a mother of four from Ecuador. **She gave so much more to me.**

It was part of my retirement strategy to be a literacy volunteer. This was something I had thought about for years yet never pursued because of the commitment and time constraints. When the email posted to my in-box with a schedule that fit my new 3-day work week, I immediately replied, "Yes!"

A flurry of emails and phone calls followed until the starting date of training arrived. That's when I learned that becoming a literacy volunteer would require 4-hour workshops, for six consecutive weeks. Really? I just wanted to be nice and volunteer. My reaction to the long haul of talking head-instructors, stream of worksheets, homework and group work was tepid.

There were about 20 of us in the class, most of them a lot older than I, all retired teachers. We all pushed through and bonded, even kept in touch afterwards.

I began to understand a motivation to volunteer: to meet new acquaintances, plus an earnest desire to help others learn to speak and read English.

The first encounter I had with Rosa was everything that I anticipated. We met at the local library. In walked a tiny young woman with her 6-year-old son already as tall as she. I towered over them and I'm only 5' 6". Rosa looked harried, tense, even timid. Her hair was a tad oily and her skin mottled with acne. I felt her anxiety and made every attempt to put mother and son at ease. We decided to sit in the children's room which suited her perfectly since she was petite and her son could browse.

We spent the first few lessons speaking in my fractured Spanish and her broken English. She was embarrassed to say anything in English. Again, I assured her the only way she would become fluent was to speak English as much as possible. I learned that she had 4 children total, two were in high school. One could only deduce that Rosa started her family as a teen-ager. There was a husband, but their extended families still lived in Ecuador. Rosa worked two jobs besides raising her children. She cleaned houses and had a business that she ran from her home. The business remained a mystery and I did not pry. I was embarrassed to let her know that I was semi-retired. I felt as if my lifestyle was carefree by comparison. Though I think she may have thought I said **tired** and not retired.

As the weeks passed, Rosa canceled some sessions, then, she asked if I could come to her house instead of meeting at the library. We had been instructed during our training never to meet students in their home or to take them in our car. I told her I was a sorry but we had to continue at the library. Besides, a goal I had set for her was to obtain a library card.

More weeks passed, Rosa's appearance improved, she was less nervous, and able to read some sight words and put together simple sentences. It was time for the library card, the passport to the world of books, magazines, and films. She brought two pieces of identification with her and borrowed a children's library book with her own card.

"Now I'm going to read with my two little younger children," she said smiling. I hugged and congratulated her. I wanted to continue to meet, but her schedule became erratic and she still wanted me to come to her home. One week passed, then three more, Rosa and I didn't meet. She and I texted back and forth. Still no day was set for our next meeting. Soon after that I sustained an injury which made me temporarily disabled. We lost touch.

Not too long ago, Rosa and I saw one another while food-shopping. We recognized each other immediately and hugged. "Yo-an," she said to me. "My English is better. Thank you."

"Yes, but thank **you** Rosa," I replied. "I am sorry if I let you down."

"No, this is good," she replied. "I am still learning with my family."

Rosa was a part of my retirement journey and she could not realize how we were both learning to be something new. Her grace meant so much to me.

The Best Day of Your Life

Write it on your heart that every day
is the best day of your life.
Emily Dickinson

Today is the best day of your life! That was a running "joke" between my former boss and me for several years. Even when the work was overwhelming, when I thought I was ready to quit, even when I felt there had to be an easier way to earn a living than to be a college financial aid counselor. I'm sure there is, as I am also sure that this day is the best day of my life, so was yesterday, and the days prior.

It just so happens to be the birthday of my former boss today and that is why I probably thought of him and our mutual mantra. The weather is sparkling with just enough chill in the air to feel refreshing. I'm sure he's having a good birthday with his wife, their son, and dog.

I decided to take a walk about town to make sure I also enjoyed this best day of my life. I had a card to drop off at the post office and went by way of a little park that is in the center of town right next to the railroad station. There is an octagon monument that I noticed for the first time with its inscriptions.

There were engraved names of fallen soldiers from our town dating back to World I, World II, Korean War, Viet Nam War, and the aftermath of September

11, 2001. These men whom I would never know gave their lives so that I can walk freely down this street, enjoy the autumn weather, and look forward to more days like this in retirement.

When they died it surely couldn't have been the best day of their lives, nor of their loved ones who mourned. This thought took the wind out of my sails and made me extremely grateful for their sacrifice. Even though I stood in the middle of town it felt like sacred ground. The earth beneath my feet was exactly where it was supposed to be, to remember these men and know that this was truly the best day of my life. Make today yours.

Your Time

Do not squander time,
for that is the stuff life is made of.
Benjamin Franklin

Time, the way I spend it, and spend time thinking about it appears to be a common thread in my life since I stopped working every day. Work allowed me to not have to think about what to do, the time was filled for me, it passed each day unnoticed until it brought me to this very day.

Perhaps as a writer my time is measured in words and the number of words I wrote that day. What is it about writers that we covet our time almost to a point of hoarding? It could be because time is an intangible, illusive, can't be banked for future use. You either utilize the time you have here and now or accept that it has been lost, slipped away, gone forever. Geeze, gone forever sounds like a death. Can time die?

Yesterday is gone, but it holds a pleasant afterglow. Walking along the Piermont jetty, soaking up the mid-afternoon sunlight and searching for driftwood were the only items on the agenda. Knowing that today would be another free day allowed me to be immersed in the riverside environment whereas previous Sundays I would mentally tick-off a Monday to-do list. My list yesterday was simply to relax and write. I sat calmly hearing the choppy Hudson River rhythmically lap against rocks and in that space I heard my own voice. One of the images I caught on camera was a woman whose bicycle was parked roadside while she sat among the warm rocks facing a quiet inlet writing in her journal. Paradise.

Yesterday is gone, today is here among the living. I am. Therefore, I write. This is what semi-retirement has afforded me. Forget the warnings of having enough money, what about your time? Taking an early retirement at 62 really means putting a claim to your time. Use it or lose it.

Paved with Gold

Trust the treasure we look for is hidden
in the ground on which we stand.
Henri J.M. Nouwen

It is a postcard autumn day, the sky is a carpet of blue, trees are bright oranges and red, a slight breeze is nature's perfect air-conditioning, and I am all set out on my walk around town. I'm wearing one of my new favorite blouses, black with white polka-dots, slimming black slacks and a slingback low-heel sandal. There is an undeniable bounce in my stride, I'm on a mission, mining for gold.

Do you recall when history teachers back in the day repeated the phrase that foreigners swore

"America's streets are paved with gold."   It's only after all these years of living here as a native, that I understand that there are golden opportunities—even in our own hometown.

I wandered up and downside streets, storefronts, visited merchants, restaurants, banks, and gift shops, pitching my husband's art for a month-long art exhibit. Perhaps garner a sale or two in the process. Well, I am happy to say that I had two serious nibbles, one person wanted to know if November would be too soon. Too soon? It's never too soon to exhibit Steve's art and possibly make money.

We shook hands and she said she would call me back before the end of the week. Hmmm, today is Wednesday, this sounded serious. She wanted to move my proposal forward not wasting a minute. My heart leapt as she handed her business card , shook my hand, and sounded as if a deal was sealed.

If I were working fulltime, I would not have had the opportunity to do this nor the energy. Being semi-retired has afforded me this gift. It is a gift to me, to have the confidence and courage to believe. You may think this is a small thing, but how many of you have decided not to attempt something out of fear?

It is so important to believe in yourself, the power of one, to not be afraid of failure. There is more fear in settling for defeat before you even made one attempt. Imagine if we all believed in ourselves, our spouses, our friends, our community, what a more beautiful and productive world we would live in. Get out there and grab your miner's hat. There's gold out there even when you're retired.

Postscript: *My husband did have the solo exhibit and was interviewed on local television. A portion of the sales went toward The American Cancer Society's Relay for Life.*

Stuck, Rooted, or Replanted

Happiness doesn't have just one address.
Anonymous

My longest sustained friendship has been with Barbara whom I met in Kindergarten. She visited me yesterday and we spent several hours chatting, walking, and browsing through a local flea market. What relaxing and uncomplicated fun we had!

For several hours we didn't speak about our adult children, global woes, not even our husbands. It was a time just for us to reminisce about our 50+ years of friendship and what we hoped for our futures.

Several years ago Barbara and her husband bought a lovely home in Florida. I almost want to label it a retirement home, but when I think about the energy that Barbara has for life, the word retirement doesn't capture her essence. But retirement did come up for both of us. I made it infinitely clear about enjoying semi-retirement, and she shared that she's been thinking lately about full retirement. She loves her professional career as an accounting professor and works hard to still connect with students who are now some 15 years younger than her own adult children. Her enthusiasm for her work is what keeps her moving forward.

The conversation inevitably turned to where she would live when retired. She expressed a slight fear that once she permanently moves to Florida, she may feel it was a mistake. As if to say, "Is that all it is?" Is that all retirement is, to move from where you had your roots for 60 years and transplant yourself to a warmer environment?

Which brings us to the concept of aging in place; staying among the familiar, where you are connected, know the back streets as well as you know the laugh lines around your mouth.

On the flipside of staying put is my daughter who longs for adventure, wants to travel, experience new venues, and use her multi-lingual gifts. She is at an age when retirement may as well be as far as Neptune. It is an alien concept as it should be, but she has learned from my example that it happens quicker than we realize. I hope that I show her that growing older and retirement should not be dreaded.

Everything has to do with outlook, and a positive outlook will help anyone of us at any point in our lives.

She expressed that she was at a crossroads in her life, but not that there wasn't an urgency to make a decision. She just didn't want to end up like her neighbors, two sisters who have lived in the same town for over 50 years. So there is a difference between being **stuck and rooted.**

We shouldn't pass judgment, but one is tempted to say that my daughter's neighbors are stuck. Both sisters are full of fear to make a move or change. I don't know what they do outside of staying home inside their apartment, going out to lunch occasionally, food-shopping, and watching television.

The times my daughter has spoken to them, they make wishful statements about wanting to move.

They're in their early 70s, but they have not set any goals for moving. Both are pleasant and love their hometown. Perhaps they are not stuck, simply rooted.

Barbara is neither. She replanted herself and re-rooted in Florida, basking in sunshine and retirement.

Sick Day

Smile, breathe and go slowly.
Thích Nhất Hạnh

I'm sick today. Some stomach virus that has knocked the stuffing out of me. While I'm alternating between dozing and staring, my thoughts are swimming and I start to wonder if it's too late for me to have a life plan.

Back in the day when I was in my forties I was a public relations director and planned many events. Birth is an unplanned event for each of us, which is followed by many milestones and events. Some planned and many others not.

Gosh, I do need a retirement life plan. I guess this has occurred to me because how quickly days pass, weeks motor through, months and seasons change without notice, and here I am at 62. Maybe I have another 12-15 good years ahead of me. Do I want to wander through them aimlessly? What do I want for myself, my husband, our children, extended family, and friends?

I don't want the days to be marked by bills paid every 30 days until the next time they're due. My overarching goal is not to leave any unpaid debt, but it has to be more than this. Much more. It was time to take an inventory of myself. Admittedly, doing it on a day that I wasn't feeling well was not the best idea.

But nothing like the present to take care of something, especially a life plan.

My first 62 years are over, at this point it doesn't matter whether they were planned or not. I didn't plan to be sick today. So the first plan of action is to feel better.

Happiness and Money

Wealth is the ability to truly experience life.
Henry David Thoreau

Every article we read today regarding retirement emphasizes money. One may ask why because money isn't necessarily the sole basis for other life-changing decisions, such as marriage, having children, or career moves. Those events also focus on emotions. Do you love him/her? Are you mature enough to have children and ready to put someone else first? Do you really want the dream job and are willing to sacrifice the demands of your time? If people did ask whether they had enough money to support a family, this world would be far less populated. So why all the monetary doom and gloom about retirement?

These were points I considered when it was time to retire:

- My health and mobility at 62 were good to enjoy activities.
- I longed for flexible days.
- I wanted to see friends more.
- The downside was no medical benefits for the next 3 years.

Do you have a personal retirement map that includes activities such as:

Mentoring, creativity, local travel, volunteering, gardening, reading, hiking, learning a new language, and continuing education? Do you like where you live? Are you ready to lead a different daily life and leave behind the job/career you have now?

If you have answered yes to many of the above then you may have a satisfying retirement. You don't need a pot of money to do any of these. Possessions may become a liability, especially if you must maintain them with repairs which require money or they accumulate the dreaded 4-letter word, dust.

Happiness has been defined by money through advertising, telling us we needed more outside of ourselves to feel complete. Happiness and money have become interchangeable just when so many of us are about to retire and enjoy the fruits of our labor.

Just to cover myself, I do advocate to save money and to be frugal. But if we wait for the perfect time to do anything, how many of us would accomplish what we have? There will never be a perfect time to retire. **If you want to retire, then the time is now.**

Catching My Breath

Time spent with a good friend
is like a dip in the Fountain of Youth.
Judy Casillo

More changes…a colleague is leaving, my daughter is moving, my husband is applying for social security, and today I met a friend whom I met more than 30 years ago for lunch. And that is a change for me now that I'm semi-retired. I made plans to meet a friend and not just sit at home writing.

We have been in each other's lives, but not where we call each other every week. Yet, there was a time when we saw each other every day when we were colleagues.

She still has beautiful curly hair, bright blue eyes, and a smile filled with her own white perfect teeth. We embrace, settle in with tea and a sandwich, and then talk and talk non-stop for two and half hours. The minutes are filled with memories, some tears, many laughs, where we've been, our children who are now grown and independent, our husbands, our other friends, movies, books, the conversation is like a fast-paced tennis match. There is not a lull in the conversation and I am as excited to hear what she has to say as much as what I have to say. I listen to her voice, really hear her words, it sounds the same as when we sat across from each other at the publishing firm years ago.

I never saw this rich friendship coming. That someday this colleague would be such an important friend in my life, and it has taken a good part of my lifetime to realize. She's been supportive going to my plays, coming to my husband's art receptions, affirming that some of my life choices weren't wrong and has enriched my life.

She arrived in her yoga outfit just after her class and I was dressed in jeans and casual blouse. There were no pretenses, we laughed at our aging hair and bodies, our faulty memories, and wrote down titles of books that each of us recommended to the other.

Our friendship has changed and evolved as all long-term relationships. She will always be Judy blue eyes to me. Like that song from the 1970s. And that was her then…and now. Love you, Judy.

An Unexpected Event

"I quit!" A colleague announced without warning.

By now I should realize nothing is constant but change. Except when it comes to unexpected changes.

A colleague of mine resigned without any notice. When she called me from her car and simply said, "Joan, I quit. I can't talk right now," it felt as if I was punched in the stomach. We had just been talking on the phone an hour earlier about the next group of students, and here she was o-u-t. We talked about meeting for lunch. I thought she was my friend. Yes, the blood bath continued with little regard to how it impacted the lives of employees and the students.

She was the last person standing in the admissions department witnessing the "grim reaper VP" appearing unannounced to colleagues' desks to escort them out of the building. She wasn't going to wait for that to happen to her.

About 5 days later she calls me again to tell me that she's walking on the beach in Florida and took another job. I was happy for her, but still shocked. She continued to say how she wasn't appreciated by her director and enumerated all the ailments of the organization I still worked for even if part-time. I am still a loyal employee.

The whole incident brought me to a dark place over the weekend. I even began to think I may have said something wrong to her. I wrestled over every word, analyzed my tone, her tone, but it still came down to the fact that she quit and it had absolutely nothing to do with me; though we did have one of those conversations just prior to her abrupt departure where people agree to disagree. This was nothing new though and I had learned to diffuse the tension with a funny comment.

So, who are your friends, and can colleagues be friends? I have become friends with colleagues along the way throughout my fulltime employment years. Some have remained my friends, others drifted. I have concluded that there are friends on the job, and friends for life, and sometimes they become both. It doesn't always happen because in some cases the glue that kept you bonded was the job. Still, I try to make new friends, different ages, different ethnicities and races, some work out and some don't. Whatever transpires after they leave, I can look back and say with confidence that I was kind to them, respectful, made them laugh, and lessened their burden at the job. Whether our paths cross again is not quite clear. What is clear is that we parted on friendly terms and left the friendship door open. This is something I have finally realized late in life: the importance to keep the door to friendship open.

Widow at Spring Tea

Widow. The word consumes itself.
Sylvia Plath

We see them everywhere, in the checkout line at stores, in church, at the library, and in my case at a happy event at a spring tea. If you're anything like me, you may have an irrational fear that what has happened to them, you will "catch." I am speaking about widowhood. For me it is a dark transition, probably because I know it means someone has died.

I envision feeling naked without my husband. How could I possibly go forward without this person with whom I have shared so many secrets, private jokes and moments, arguments, tears, all that is intimate in any authentic relationship? Life and living become a challenge from the mundane waking in the morning, to the more complex and adventurous solo travel, and everything between.

There was Mary at the spring tea, an animated lady of seventy-something who attended with her forty-year-old daughter. I already had circulated enough with others, enjoyed delicious scones, assorted pastries, and breads, shared stories and laughs, when I decided to settle in an empty chair next to Mary. She and her daughter were discussing the costs of cable television and the myriad of viewing options we now have with another forty-something lady. Before long the topic drifted between the young women, I lost interest, and turned to Mary. Someone had mentioned PBS, and I thought this might be the direction to go.

There was an instant connection when we both agreed that we were satisfied having watched "Upstairs Downstairs" years ago and saw no need to get hooked-on "Downton Abbey." Mary was clearly a full decade older than I, but we have found common ground. We discovered that both our husbands are artists. Well Mary's was, but he had passed away two years ago.

So, a topic that I feared the most I decided to broach with Mary. I asked her gently how was life without her husband? Is it worse, how does she manage? I could tell she welcomed the questions and was at a point in her grieving to be able to share and talk unemotionally and honestly.

"Well, first let me say that I was always at my husband's side," then added, "and in his shadow. When people heard that he was an artist and worked for the NY Times, all the attention immediately turned to him. He loved it. I was proud of him and basked in the attention he received, but I was sort of invisible."

She spoke intelligently, softly, occasionally touching my arm, which was endearing. I don't recall the color of her eyes. She was plain in her appearance and her bare face was a spotted and creased canvass revealing the years that passed. This was a woman who had lived, loved, had children, grandchildren, friends, a husband, and now was a widow. Mary inspired me to be more of me, not to be afraid of aging, to wear it like a crown of achievement.

"Being a widow is different," she said. "Neither better nor worse. But staying home day after day is certainly a recipe for depression." Mary's strategy to avoid depression is to belong to a world affairs group, a political group, a knitting group, and spending time at the senior center in town.

Soon afterwards I left the spring tea vowing all the way home that when I saw my husband I would embrace him and tell him how much I cared. That night before I fell asleep I thought about Mary. What about when the lights go out, and the pillow next to

you is empty? Who do you kiss good night? I leaned
over and kissed my husband.

A Swing and a Miss

*After all, the wrong road
always leads somewhere.*
George Bernard Shaw

For two years now I have wanted to revel at an Oktoberfest. Not a drop of me is German, nor is my husband. But just like on St. Patrick 's Day we're *Irish*, why not be German for a day? I wanted to hear an oompah band, raise a glass of brew, eat some knockwurst, and just take a step outside of my Italian-American traditions.

Well, it will have to wait for another year, I think. We trekked up to Bear Mountain only to find that thousands of other people also wanted to enjoy a quintessential autumn Sunday, leaving us on an endless trail of bumper-to-bumper traffic and no way to turn around. We inched our way to the entrance only to find that there was no more available parking anywhere…and drove home.

We spent two hours of our lives in the car filled with hope and a few laughs on the return. In a way we had arrived. What does this have to do with retirement? Plenty. Choose your activities carefully and plan early.

The Joy of Finding Identity

Know thyself.
Ancient Greek saying.

This week my work schedule was turned around and in the process I have confused some of my colleagues. Tomorrow when I return to work they'll think it may be Thursday and the next day Friday. They will be disappointed to find out that Thursday I'll be out and it is not the end of the week. The switch in days made me discombobulated. I see now how easy I have slipped into a comfortable routine of Monday and Wednesdays away from the office. Today I have even had trouble settling down to write. Besides, I'm a bit depressed, not motivated to do anything. And yet I have so much to be thankful for.

I talk to myself and say, "Damn it, Joan, stop being depressed. What the hell is the matter now?" *I thought I was doing the retirement thing correctly.*

Again it was time to have a chat day I myself. "So who are you, Joan?"

I cringe to think I may have come this far not knowing myself or who I am. But it is true, lately I feel like I'm harboring a stranger inside of me. I decided to have a face-to-face meeting with *her* in front of the bathroom mirror.

Let me out.

"Just a minute while I'll find the key, what did you say your name is?"

Joan. J-o-a-n.

"The Joan I knew who went to work Monday through Friday. She sat at various desks throughout her life, once had a corner office with two windows. That Joan?"

Yes big deal. Look around the apartment. You have dozens of windows now.

"The same Joan who was out the door almost every weekday at 8 o'clock in the morning? The same Joan who made colleagues laugh and offered emotional support? That same, Joan?"

Your point?

I stare in the mirror, it's me all right.

"Hello me."

Remember, there are no rules for retirement. Joan, you are who you have always been, only now you're not working fulltime.

You may or may not struggle with your purpose, calling and identity as much as I have. But with retirement there may be some questions directed inward. You will have the answers for you. Today I rediscovered the "I" in identity. And so the journey continued.

How Old Do You Feel?

Aging is not lost youth, but a new stage of opportunity and strength.
Betty Friedan

While at a recent cocktail party, a woman who looked older than I came right out and asked if I was retired. The question jolted me. I felt as if she had made a judgment on my appearance. But on another level I felt old, past it, outdated, a relic who had been invited to the event to offset the 30-somethings.

I quickly replied, "Oh no, I'm still working." As if work would validate my existence and my right to be an attendee. I even went as far to ask her, "Do I look that old?" She assured me I did not. So why didn't she just ask me where I worked?

I was both surprised by her question and more so at my reaction. Why did it make me uncomfortable? Wasn't this what I wanted? And here is the rub, whether you or I want it, sooner or later we will be older and old, and it may become a frequent question. I have to learn how to field queries about my employment status with grace, enthusiasm, and confidence. Why?

Yes, why do I suddenly feel the need to defend my status as part-time retiree? I recall a close relative of mine who barked at anyone who dared to ask him if he was enjoying retirement. Several years later, he brags about it.

Honesty

Three things cannot be long hidden:
the sun, the moon, and the truth.
Buddha

Speaking my mind ... me and my big mouth! Uh-oh, it's happened to me. I took part in a group interview where we asked questions of an applicant. Her personality flat lined, her smile which was barely evident appeared forced. She didn't elaborate on the answers just merely replied in simple sentences. Her demeanor could be interpreted by nervousness, or she thought the job would be hers just for showing up, or she was genuinely not interested in the position. Whatever it was, we decided unanimously we weren't interested in her. Then just before I dropped the other shoe, or perhaps a bomb, our director asked what we thought of her. I shot out, "That was the most painful interview I have ever sat through." Honestly. It had dragged on for more than an hour with little information about who the applicant was. Except all my young colleagues were aghast at my blunt reply. They sort of laughed, but also said "Joan!"

Well go Joan yourself, I say. Let's not mince words. The one thing I have learned in my 62 years is to speak honestly and feel honestly. And if these little darlings who have to be politically correct all the time don't like it, they can go ahead hide their true feelings or sugar coat them to please themselves and eventually see how it will make them feel inauthentic.

OK, so here I am authentic self, semi-retired, and I'm not going to lie, I felt dumb right after I shot from the hip. I felt old. I felt the need to express myself with a display of the better communication skills I have been blessed with. Too late. Did you hear the buzzer? The floor was grabbed by one of the youngins who said, "Oh she was immature," and all the others chimed in with that. Truth, none of us were impressed with the applicant. But I was the least impressed and succinctly vocal about it. Now that doesn't sound too dumb.

Retirement takes pulling weeds because the season is short and you only want the best in you to bloom. To blossom you must be honest with yourself and others.

You're Just…

Turn your face toward the sun
and the shadows will fall behind you.
Maori Proverb

I had an encounter with a VP at my office. Without going into detail about what transpired, his parting words to me were, "You're just a part-time worker."

What a kick in the teeth. I intuitively felt that this had more to do with my status as a semi-retired **woman**. His remark made me feel dumb, old, and unimportant. That my opinion didn't matter anymore, or that the knowledge I possessed and skills that I have were no longer valued. What is my added value, what is the benefit of keeping me employed here? He knew but chose to let me know it didn't matter.

The week before I had another punch in the stomach when a colleague of mine just up and quit. What gives at this place? Has anyone at the workplace made you feel this way either subtly or overtly?

The students whom I service have always found me efficient, personable, and caring. I have written articles where I have shed the spotlight on the college. I talk up the school whenever I am given a chance. How I was discarded as "just a part-time worker" widened the abyss where I had one foot in work and another in retirement. I felt my self-esteem dissolve. *Nobody is just any one thing,* I grumbled to myself. Mister VP.

Now repeat after me I said: *I am a multifaceted, multitalented lady who is liked and respected, even loved. Get off your throne, Mr. VP and thank the little people here who uphold our organization's mission, work hard, even harder with shorter hours. Don't be so quick to dismiss us.*

I never said those words to him. He avoided me for many months. At what would be my last college Christmas party he sat keeping a low profile. I calmly walked toward him, shook his hand wishing him a Merry Christmas. My small act of kindness felt good. His shadow fell behind me.

The Meeting

Don't cry because it's over.
Smile because it happened.
Dr. Seuss

It was a day I welcomed, expected, and dreaded. The part-time hours at the college had reached a dead end. Enrollment had dropped so much that I was not needed even part-time. My boss had told me up front when he agreed to let me work part-time that my post may actually come to an end within a year. And it did.

The Friday when I was called into the VP's office for "the meeting" was a beautiful spring day just weeks before May graduation. My boss drove me across campus and would sit-in on the meeting. There was a quiet almost solemn atmosphere that surrounded the three of us once the VP's office was closed. The end was really going to happen, my thoughts were spinning from anxiety and this is how it happens when you're 62 and an employer deems your position as unnecessary.

I've sat in chairs like this before, so many times before, the desks, the blotters, the clocks, the family pictures all look the same. I have heard "you're hired" "congratulations on a project well done" "you have a raise" and now after 46 years of employment, I had reached the end of my journey. It was almost exactly one year to the day when my part-time hours began that I was officially given notice of my departure.

My boss wanted me to work through June, but I felt that the end of the spring semester in May just after graduation made more sense. Negotiation for severance and unemployment followed, and that was it. Just like the film "About Schmidt" I gathered my belongings which were few, and every day until I reached May 8, 2015, I worked toward cleaning files, contacting students, and keeping my boss informed of any issues.

A couple of days before my official leave, the team gave me a farewell luncheon with good food, funny stories, and a book where everyone wrote how they enjoyed working with me for the past 7 years.

That's when I realized there's no going back. That night I stared into the darkness of my bedroom and thought about it all. I visualized several farewell luncheons, former co-workers, bosses, companies. I could no longer think, *I'll go back there to work someday, or maybe there is an opening at that place I liked*. It was over.

I felt strongly that my fulltime employment had truly come to an end. Self-employment is altogether something different, but what company, organization, or school would hire a woman of 62 for a fulltime job with benefits? But the question for me was: what 62-year-old woman in her right mind would look for a fulltime job? Fulltime work was over, but a new season has just begun.

We're Not Evergreens

These are the days that must happen to you.
Walt Whitman

It came from out of left field when I discovered that two people I assumed were still living had died. One passed this May 2015, the other in October 2011. The former was a first cousin of mine who lived in Boston all his life and died at the age of 70. I am 63. The latter was a man that I dated for a short time in my forties. He collapsed while jogging and died on a high school track at the age of 65.

The other passing that I face is what I call "the long good-bye." My former sister-in-law, the sister of my first husband, my daughter's aunt. She was diagnosed with cancer and dementia about 8 years ago, and both have progressed. The cancer slowly, the dementia not so. She was a beautiful brilliant poised articulate woman whose persona has been chipped away to child-like interactions.

The jogger once told me that his father dropped dead just after a Passover dinner when he was 60 years old. My reaction was that his father had been taken too soon. The time this was shared with me I was in my forties. The jogger's response was, "No, he died just on time."

We come from different perspectives, different ages, different ailments, and all will eventually pass. It is a reminder that there are days that must be. You must do things while you can. That is why I have chosen to start my path to retirement when I did.

A New Beginning

We're always the same age inside.
Gertrude Stein

As mentioned earlier, I was hired as a Library Page at the Pearl River Public library. In my element for sure, working with others who love to read, talk about movies, local events, grandkids, gardening, and life! As I carefully shelve books, I am armed with a paper and pencil to jot down titles that interest me. So far I have read a book every week, plus the one for the book club, plus my own writing. Bliss.

It's only 7-10 hours a week, adds structure to my week, I have contact with new faces, little children, and can make suggestions to patrons who are looking for a good book to read.

I have so many plans for this summer and fall. I want to take a continuing education course, walk the High Line in New York City, and attend an upcoming high school reunion. I feel like that lady in the Medicare commercial who is happily walking in the woods and announces, "I'm only in my sixties, I have big plans and a long life ahead of me."

Well, not so fast…

Humbled

Into each life some rain must fall.
Henry Wadsworth Longfellow

It was a golden sun-drenched August morning, reminiscent of a summer day in my youth. My husband and I rolled out of bed, ate our oatmeal, and decided an early walk would be a perfect way to start the day. To be honest I had a touch of vertigo when I opened my eyes, a condition that every once in awhile ruins part or all of my day. A strong cup of coffee would remedy it quickly, I was sure, and it did.

Now there had been a spat of broken arms and legs, fractured and twisted ankles among staff at the library since I started working. In fact, the night before when I was at work my supervisor informed me that Kelly had fallen while on vacation and hurt her back. I half-joked, "Gee, I hope this isn't catchy."

"I think we need an exorcism," my supervisor said half-seriously.

When my husband and I ventured outside for a walk, I prayed silently, pleading with God not to make me fall. About 30 minutes into the walk, I fell and fractured my ankle.

Never in my life had I been disabled for several weeks. The only way I could navigate was on crutches or hopping on one foot. My husband was a wreck. Everything that I normally did or took care of fell on his shoulders: the food-shopping, the laundry, meals, fed the cats and cleaned the litter box, helped me take a shower, tossed the trash, and recyclables, did all the driving. And because we live in an upstairs apartment with many stairs down to the main entrance and more stairs to the parking area, I lie on the couch day-after-day with my injured foot elevated, reading, sleeping, and thinking.

My mind went to dark places. I visually scanned the apartment thinking this is how it will be when I'm gone. Stuff remains, inanimate objects rule, and once deceased it will not matter whether I ever purchased the wide-screen television, new curtains, went to Scotland or stayed home. Nothing mattered. That is, the only thing that mattered or would make a difference was to have health.

I repeated my husband's healing prayer three times each day and promised God that when I was healed I would do good deeds for other people to show my gratitude. I would reach out to others, some whom I have neglected.

What also struck me was that retirement was going to be a mixed experience just as life had always been. It's not as if one fades into the sunset with a perpetual smile, endless luncheons. No matter what big plans you may have, if you're in your sixties or seventies, existence has a way of reminding us that we're not always in control, and that our bodies will continue to change through aging. And having this perspective is wisdom.

230

Your Legacy

*I meditate on all your works and
consider what your hands have done.*
Psalm 143.5

Were you told if you did a good job you would be
rewarded but found along the proverbial corporate
ladder it didn't always work that way? I didn't make it
to "the top" but I worked conscientiously and with
kindness each step of the way.

I have been reflecting about my employment, all
the employment, all the employers, the bosses, the
coworkers, the companies, and frankly I am amazed
how I survived it all. Aren't you sometimes impressed
how you have kept your sanity, and level headedness

while facing unrealistic deadlines, too much work, demanding supervisors, and if you worked with the public you can add that as an extra merit badge.

Why did we accept it without considering an alternative? Part of the reason has been that many of us used the model of working for someone else, a bigger entity. The Internet and online businesses were non-existent.

I never thought about retirement until reaching sixty. Can retirement really be the brass ring we want as we spin on the employment merry-go-round? It is if you retire relatively healthy and not in debt. But even if you are neither, retirement isn't a negative, view it as rewarding yourself after many years of work.

What is my employment legacy? As a public relations director for a national emergency organization I worked tirelessly through 911 and other major disasters; was a solid magazine content editor; and a peerless college financial aid counselor. None of these can be quantified.

My legacy is an intangible. I was merely the vessel that others saw. My legacy was the working journey which helped others, listened, empathized, and tossed in humor to smooth the bumps.

Your legacy may be more prestigious and innovative. You were a change maker, you taught the next generation, you served justice for those whose voice was silenced. Regardless, consider retirement and how a new legacy is possible.

Letting Go

When I let go of what I am,
I become what I might be.
Lao Tzu

Now one of my first tasks in full retirement has been to organize, clean, and streamline. Why? Hadn't I had enough of organization for the past 40 years in one way or another? Maintaining press releases, files, databases, desk drawers, projects—enough already!

So, my personal belongings suffered through the years with neglect because I was tired from work and household chores. Evening was my time to relax with a book and television. Out of sight, out of mind, was my silent mantra and code of conduct each day I returned home from the office.

When I began to seriously tackle drawers and paperwork, I was astounded how much of it I really didn't want to keep. The shredder came in handy, and I was considerate not to do it when my husband was home. The cats learned to deal with the grinding; in fact, the constant drone became white noise that put them to sleep. Streams of memos, letters, cards, date books, and scraps with scribbled phone numbers and names were swallowed into oblivion. It was a catharsis.

When you begin weeding, you may realize as I did that you start to make decisions both unconsciously and consciously what to let go. I'm not going to lie and say that it is easy, but it is freeing. And in the process I realize that I may have to let go of some relationships and which will always remain important. You will let go of some clothes that you may have clung to because you loved the way they made you look and feel, yet those clothes are for the past. Schedules and appointments that once caused you worry, are past as well. Today is the day you are living right now.

Mothers & Daughters
Part I

*And it is still true, that woman
will mother no one until she too is born.
American-Indian proverb*

When was the last time you thought about your mother? For me hardly a day passes. What about your grandmother? And if you have children, you think of them all the time. Retirement may bring these thoughts. How similar and how different our lives have been in 4 generations. Today, I feel as if I am holding the hand of my mother and daughter. I am a link in a chain of womanhood.

It is interesting how sometimes mothers and daughters run parallel lives. My daughter who is in her thirties recently had a disagreement with one of her oldest friends. She and I spoke about it at length and I encouraged her to keep in contact with her friend, this happens in any long-term relationship. Her girlfriend texted her and suggested they talk the next day and they will.

The previous day, a friend of mine called to share how she had a cardiac catheterization and that it didn't go well. Not only the findings, but the aftermath of a hematoma and feeling very unwell, tired, and discouraged. She has always been perky, spirited, and an inspiration about going forward while shadows surrounded her. Hers is a very long-term friendship that I am not prepared to lose.

And so I spoke with my daughter about it, and I related not only about my friend, but how her father years ago had lost his longtime chess friend. And I didn't understand the magnitude of the loss. We simply can't replace friends, we may acquire new ones if we're lucky enough to find someone we want to nurture a friendship with, but never can we replace the loss of a lifelong friend.

So my daughter encouraged me to see my friend as much as possible and be there for her. And in that moment my daughter also had an "ah-ha" moment. She and her friend will speak, and the friendship will continue...

Mothers & Daughters
Part II

My Mother

*When I stopped seeing my mother
through the eyes of a child; I saw the woman
who helped me give birth to myself.*
Nancy Friday

Mom. I would be remiss for me not to mention her. Maybe you thought about your mom while reading through my retirement journey. Was (or is) your mother an influence in the career path you chose?

She worked fulltime since I was two. My mother planted the seeds of employment outside the home when most women stayed at home and ran the household.(She did all that as well.) To be a "stay at home mom" seemed like a luxury for her because my father was beset by many *illnesses* too often to hold a job for long. That was the family story. The script my brothers and I all accepted in our youth. That story crumbled when mom was diagnosed with terminal cancer 3 years after she retired.

I was a pest. There was mom preparing for work while her little daughter stood next to her, hogging the mirror to put on pretend lipstick. I emulated her. I even blotted my make-believe lipstick with a tissue. When she combed her hair, I brushed my tangled curls; when she sprayed her hair, I made believe I was using hairspray all the while underfoot and chattering nonsense. My little heart wanted her to stay home.

She soldiered on for the next 37 years of my life. I learned to appreciate who she was, the work she did, the skills she had, the position she garnered at 62 years old as Deputy Surrogate of Bergen County, New Jersey. She was the first woman in the history of Bergen County to hold that title. What a coup for a woman from her generation.

Mom most definitely influenced me to have a college education, to have a career...or several as was my journey. In fact, sometimes I refer to myself as "The Serial Employee." I was different from my mom, I was from post-World War II generation, a Baby Boomer. The foundation she laid was set otherwise.

A phone call I received from mom while working crushed me to the core. She called me with shocking news about her terminal illness. I could not stop crying. I was a mess in a public place. I tried to conceal myself in the cubicle. Nothing made sense anymore. I called my sister-in-law who at the time was working at a marketing firm just across the street. We met outside, she placed her arm around my shoulder, my knees buckled. I was sobbing…

One year later, mom was gone. Her legacy of a strong work ethic influenced all her children. Her passing signaled to me how fast life was. It was then when I decided not to wait until 67 to fully retire.

Being The Retired Mom

There are only two lasting bequests
we can hope to give our children.
One of these is roots, the other wings.
Goethe

Have you attempted to navigate your child through their career? Rushed to give advice when the workplace has changed dramatically from when you worked 40 years ago?

Maybe a half-century ago? I'm guilty. Pointing to offices and "real jobs" as the way to go; or teach at a college. These have been my go-to messages without the knowledge of how these working environments have changed. It's a whole new employment world out there.

A writer was born the first time I saw my daughter sitting in front of a typewriter in 1985. It was bright blue with a shiny silver return handle and reminded me of the Sears Citation model my parents bought for my tenth birthday. The typewriter was my parents' way of providing a future career path for me as a secretary. They of course wanted me to go to college, but you never know typing can always come in handy for a woman. Indeed it did and has, just as typing and knowing computer applications have helped my daughter in her career path.

Like my mom, I have been working with an outdated mindset. I always encouraged my daughter to be a writer and editor. It was a profession which was said to be one of the few during The Great

Depression still able to make a living. In my mind, to be a writer was a calling, having honorable employment, being creative, and expressing your voice indelibly on a page.

I always encouraged my daughter to be a writer, especially when the internet evolved creating millions of venues and possibilities to write. Blogs, self-publishing, website content, marketing, online magazines, and, and, and the reality has become virtual.

Hyperlinks, key words, social media, specific formats, and word counts are just a few of the demands placed upon freelance writers. Forget creativity.

My daughter and I don't butt heads. I have learned to respect her life path and she understands mine.

Her path is not the same as mine, never will be, and this is a positive. She has found success as a writer and editor while pursuing what speaks to her such as environmental stewardship, holistic health, and science. These subjects were not in my writer vocabulary until now.

The way we were employed was not like the previous generation. The way we retire today is not the way our parents retired and will not be anything like the next generation. Knowing this, the following poem is for my daughter.

Child of Mine

You have soared
above the cosmos
alongside shooting stars
with streaming meteor showers
and sunlit pools of sky.

Yesterday, you were a girl beside me
filled with wonder and awe.
Each step forward
led to your own path unknown,
filled with crossroads, curved and rough
sloping sharply off to nowhere
with no compass but your faith.

A map was offered.
But could my map help you
find your blueprints,
your dreams, your talents, your purpose?

Onward you persevered and pursued
your place in this universe.
You are the woman only you can be.
Uniquely lovely, amazingly wise,
and wonderfully gracious.
I applaud you.
You inspire me.
I love you.

I'm Gone

*One's destination is never a place
but rather a new way of looking at things.*
Henry Miller

Today was the first day after leaving the post as a financial aid counselor. I decided to send an email to my work address just to see what response I would receive. A few minutes later a return reply appeared informing me the email address had been disabled. I quietly read and re-read the message imagining how my former students will feel when their emails were returned. *What do you mean, isn't Joan at the college anymore? I had a question for her. Now who do I contact?*

But for me the return email was another reminder and confirmation that I was no longer employed where I required an email address associated with an organization or company. I was out on my own, a sole entity in the vast cosmos. My email had been disabled, ended, and turned-off with a click, gone. I don't know why I did this to myself. Of course my work email had to be discontinued. But who am I now?

Figuring out who we are is a lifelong process, understanding why we're here is not the same question, yet we know they are intertwined with the overall complexity of identity. Am I making this sound so academic and esoteric? Maybe it is.

I know that I have never been my jobs because my employment has been a patch quilt of careers which were done well but ultimately never lasted more than 5- 7 years each. Because the truth, my truth, is that I am a writer whose skill of communication helped me in teaching, publishing, public relations, and financial aid counseling. Never mind the adage "you are what you eat." I say, "We are what we speak and write."

These days I have more time to write poems about natural surroundings, mail cards and letters where I express my love and appreciation of friendship. If this is how *I'm gone*, then alas I have arrived.

Let the fun begin!

What a wonderful life I've had!
I only wish I'd realize it soon!
Colette

Today I am 23,258 days young/old and counting!

This is a new season! We haven't made it to a finish line because life is not a race. And we're not all going to spend our retirement years the same. I have a friend who has applied for a Master's in Fine Arts in Iowa; another who is taking a music course that she has always wanted to for years; my sister-in-law volunteers as a swimming instructor for children, and enjoys her gardening of vegetables, plants, and flowers; and another friend who enjoys helping her children with baby-sitting, and more church activities. I have a friend who is in her 80s and co-publishes a monthly magazine with her husband. She tells me the secret to a good retirement is never to stop working. But the key to her success is while in the process of publishing an informative magazine she has remained curious about life and keeps learning.

These are not all extraordinary activities, but they are pursuits these women have not had the time to do while working fulltime, traveling on business, and conducting the myriad of tasks that working women do in addition to their employment.

The Big Move

2019 - Present

Truth: Not everyone chooses after retirement to move far away from longstanding friendships, close family ties. Then only to struggle through feelings of displacement, a stranger to everyone, even yourself. This is exactly what we did in 2019.

Retirement evolved to a life I never imagined: Florida. Grandchildren were high on my list against a move to Florida. Next, was my irrational belief that alligators roamed freely on every street and appeared in your toilet when you were in a vulnerable position. More importantly, parting from lifelong friends, new library colleagues that I enjoyed, and membership to a church which became my spiritual home.

Friends, colleagues, and family wished us well. There were numerous farewell luncheons, dinners, teas, and gifts. All of this was emotionally overwhelming which had me constantly asking my husband was he sure he wanted to move. His reasons based on health were logical except for my having to leave the library and moving far away from family and friends. There were, however, two people already residing in Florida who accented the positive every step of the way: my daughter, and a lifelong friend I have known since kindergarten. They both assured me neither one had seen one alligator and to stop with my silly fear. Well, within three months of our arrival, there was two alligators in the community lake. We had moved to the jungle.

Truth: I was not financially or emotionally ready to stop working when employment at the college came to its inevitable ending. Simultaneously I understood how fulltime employment had become a burden to my physical and mental health. Work as a financial aid counselor involved daily email, faxes, phone calls, data input, numerous computer applications, meetings, filing, the handling of important financial documents from students and their parents, passwords to federal databases, refunds, and monitoring course credit ratio to federal financial aid acceptability. The barrage of numbers and names became mind-numbing. It was time to reinvent myself once more. You may have already recognized your own ongoing metamorphoses during retirement.

More truth: The part-time Library Page job was mine for the next four years and helped sustain us. In fact, I would still be employed there except for having moved 1300 miles away in 2019.

Relocation to another part of the country will most definitely transform your retirement. However, circumstances both health and the cost of apartments were the catalysts to our decision to move.

An affordable 2-bedroom/2-bathroom lakefront apartment in Florida became available within one month of our applying. Our move was a gunshot in the dark because we had not seen inside the apartment except virtually.

Our car was loaded with clothing, kitchenware, linens, books, my husband's art supplies and some of his art, tools, my unpublished manuscripts, boxes of photo albums, and important documents. The compact Subaru resembled something out of *The Beverly Hillbillies* sitcom. The car was stuffed with no view except for the front windshield and the sideview mirrors. Miraculously we were never stopped by police while driving south on I-95.

April through October 2019 I felt displaced for months. Depression and guilt were my two best buddies. Even with the reduced rent, we were struggling. There were costs we had not known about such as registering our vehicle in a new state would be around $800; paying an upfront premium for utilities; and food was considerably more expensive. I attempted to downplay the negative, and audaciously agreed to be interviewed by a freelance writer friend who penned what became a popular human-interest story. She wrote about us, how a retired couple with social security and small pensions were able to move to Florida. Then a miracle happened which took my retired existence on a different trajectory.

A newspaper editor I worked with in Westchester, New York, recommended me to a publisher in Vero Beach. It was an ordinary weeknight. My husband and I were watching a DVD on my old laptop when an unknown New York number appeared on my mobile phone. Maybe it was someone I knew. On the other end was a vibrant woman's voice, a publisher of local

Treasure Coast magazines who needed a content editor as soon as possible if not sooner. Hardly any words were spoken. I did not catch her name right away, I felt hired based just on the recommendation. "It's $400 for each magazine, is that okay?" *OF COURSE!* Not only did it improve our income, but it improved our outlook in these fresh surroundings.

The position allowed me to breathe and appreciate the natural beauty that surrounded us in Florida. Writing and editing for the magazine enabled us to do an Indian River pontoon ride and visit a botanical garden just a mile from our door. We were a 3-mile car ride away from the beaches. I chased butterflies and species of birds new to me, capturing the images and I was able to make several new acquaintances and learn Mahjong. I resigned from the magazine employment after nearly two years. It had begun to demand more of my *retirement* time.

Hurricane Dorian gave us a serious scare in 2019. But much more frightening events were on the way for 2020. Just a week after my March birthday, the Covid pandemic hit and we all know the tragedies which unfolded. Then in April 2020, while driving, an elderly driver was unable to stop for a red traffic signal and sped through the intersection. I was moving through the intersection with a steady green light…crash. Struck with such force that my car spun around in the opposite direction. I recall thinking, *This is how it is when you die, blacked-out and unconscious.*

The car was totaled, I sustained a concussion that caused difficulty in memory, carrying on a conversation, and severe headaches. There I was sitting in *paradise* with lockdowns, no car, and a concussion. I was fortunate to survive to the other side of the car crash and the pandemic.

The following are two experiences which filled me with joy despite the pandemic. I experienced intense well-being, cheerfulness, and renewed purpose.

Joy in Butterfly Meditation

*Walk as if you are kissing
the earth with your feet.*
Thich Nhat Hanh

To be free as a butterfly, how wonderful! During social distancing the Vero Beach Environmental Learning Center reminded me that one of the safest places to be is outside in natural surroundings. This helped me move from indoor doldrums to experience the freedom of walkways and gardens. Without hesitation, I decided to participate in a butterfly meditation. Being semi-retired afforded me the time to do this, in addition to share it with readers of the two magazines which I contributed.

It was an ideal July morning, overcast and comfortable temperatures with no threat of rain. A neighbor and I went together where we met at the entrance and were led into an expanse, followed a dirt path, and to a private area. Betty, the 90-something neighbor, a retiree, used a walker navigating eagerly to have a new experience. Deep shade and seclusion engulfed us. My quarantined senses began to sing.

We were told to empty our minds, to focus on exactly where we were. Forget the laundry, the bills, what's for dinner, instead be aware of the enormity of the fact that we were standing on planet earth! With each step, we said aloud, "I am here."

These words were repeated with each step we took while walking in a circle around the garden. We eventually made our way to the area of departure. We fell silent, simply listening to random bird calls, and spotting two butterflies. The meditation was truly refreshing.

I later learned that a butterfly has a short life-span, ranging from two weeks to 2-4 months. You wouldn't think that while observing one on wing. They appear happy, delicate, strong, and beautiful. The way a caterpillar becomes a butterfly, so can we transform ourselves during retirement. Unlike the caterpillar we may over think the process, a caterpillar simply becomes what it is meant to be. Here I was sharing the same space at the same moment with this colorful insect. The probability of our paths crossing cannot be calculated. Chance? Destiny? I accepted it as a sign of my own transformation.

Indian River Lagoon

It was magical, a chilly 52 degrees morning in Florida! The moment I stepped onto the pontoon I felt as if Eden was found. A vivid blue sky stretched beyond the imagination; birds circling above, sparse cloud formations overhead, and the sound of the water rippling against the pontoon completely enveloped me in Vero Beach's natural surroundings.

Again, I was able to do this during the pandemic because it was outdoors and write about it for the magazine as a contributor. If I had not been semi-retired, this opportunity would not have occurred. The cost for this was zero.

The pontoon guide explained the lagoon stretches seven miles and is two miles wide, crosses two weather zones: the sub-tropical and temperate. Dolphins leapt, herons and pelicans flew nearby. As vast as the water-way appeared it did not exceed more than 5-feet in depth. The guide in his closing remarks stressed harmony, protection of indigenous wildlife and hoped we would feel the importance as stewards of nature.

More than a year and half later, after healing from a concussion, I kayaked alone on the Indian River. What a thrill and exhilaration.

I recognized the similarity to being the steward of one's retirement. To make it an oasis as much as possible. You may not live lakeside, or with an ocean view, or see a mountain in the distance from your window. See what is in front of you and make it beautiful. Have potted plants, a little garden, a circle of friends, borrow books, movies, and music from your local library, practice meditation, do a crossword, ride a bicycle, walk around your community, watch a sunrise, a moonrise, a sunset. Most of all be a steward of your mind, body, and soul.

Nothing like the Present

The ship has sailed for thinking I should have found fulltime employment at 62. This is not the time to speak regrets about relocation. This is not the time to even think *I told you so.*

I have my health, peace of mind, a clearer vision for the future. The time is mine without any fulltime or part-time work. It is time to sink my teeth into reading books…and to write.

Mom said, "When you have your health, you have everything." She always placed a higher value on health. Your body is a temple which needs proper nutrition and exercise. It will carry and nourish your soul through retirement. **Begin.**

About the author

Joan B. Reid has written plays, poetry, cozy mysteries, and essays. She was a contributor to *The Bicycle Book: Wit Wisdom & Wanderings* where six of her "Life is a Bike" essays were published. Her "Life is a Bike" column appeared in numerous publications nationwide, online, and in the UK. Her play, "The Jobless Chronicle" won best play in the Monologue Mania Competition at the Producer's Club in NYC. Joan's essays and education pieces have appeared in *Art News, The Record, The Italian Tribune, Nyack Villager Magazine, The Journal News-Westchester, NY, One Voice, Student Aid Transcript, and 53rd Neighbors.*

She and her husband, Steve Reid, an artist, are retired and reside in Florida. For more details visit: Joan's View (joansview-jbreid.blogspot.com).

Thank you for reading!

Made in the USA
Middletown, DE
15 October 2021

50398160R00156